Science Libraries in the Self-Service Age

T0383237

CHANDOS
INFORMATION PROFESSIONAL SERIES

Series Editor: Ruth Rikowski
(Email: Rikowskigr@aol.com)

Chandos' new series of books is aimed at the busy information professional. They have been specially commissioned to provide the reader with an authoritative view of current thinking. They are designed to provide easy-to-read and (most importantly) practical coverage of topics that are of interest to librarians and other information professionals. If you would like a full listing of current and forthcoming titles, please visit www.chandospublishing.com.

New authors: we are always pleased to receive ideas for new titles; if you would like to write a book for Chandos, please contact Dr. Glyn Jones on g.jones.2@elsevier.com or telephone + 44 (0) 1865 843000.

Science Libraries in the Self-Service Age

Developing New Services, Targeting New Users

ALVIN HUTCHINSON

Smithsonian Libraries, Washington, DC, USA

Chandos Publishing is an imprint of Elsevier
50 Hampshire Street, 5th Floor, Cambridge, MA 02139, United States
The Boulevard, Langford Lane, Kidlington, OX5 1GB, United Kingdom

Notices

Knowledge and best practice in this field are constantly changing. As new research and
experience broaden our understanding, changes in research methods, professional practices, or
medical treatment may become necessary.

Practitioners and researchers must always rely on their own experience and knowledge in
evaluating and using any information, methods, compounds, or experiments described herein.
In using such information or methods they should be mindful of their own safety and the safety
of others, including parties for whom they have a professional responsibility.

To the fullest extent of the law, neither the Publisher nor the authors, contributors, or editors,
assume any liability for any injury and/or damage to persons or property as a matter of products
liability, negligence or otherwise, or from any use or operation of any methods, products,
instructions, or ideas contained in the material herein.

British Library Cataloguing-in-Publication Data
A catalogue record for this book is available from the British Library

Library of Congress Cataloging-in-Publication Data
A catalog record for this book is available from the Library of Congress

ISBN: 978-0-08-102033-3

For information on all Chandos Publishing publications
visit our website at https://www.elsevier.com/books-and-journals

Working together
to grow libraries in
developing countries

www.elsevier.com • www.bookaid.org

Publisher: Glyn Jones
Acquisition Editor: Glyn Jones
Editorial Project Manager: Thomas Van Der Ploeg
Production Project Manager: Joy Christel Neumarin Honest Thangiah
Cover Designer: Greg Harris

Typeset by MPS Limited, Chennai, India

DEDICATION

Dedicated to my wife and son who endured my frequent disappearances to write this book. Also to the Smithsonian Institution about which I would echo the old saying, "Find a job you love and you'll never work a day in your life."

CONTENTS

CHAPTER 1

A Self-Service Story

Disruption (like Google Scholar) can be responded to in several different ways but the only viable response from an academic library is service innovation.

Yeh and Walter (2016)

Like all service organizations in the digital era, libraries have been facing disruptive forces. What Clay Christensen called "disruptive innovation" and Joseph Schumpeter called "creative destruction" can used to describe the effects of networked information technology on libraries over the last 20 years. But libraries were not the first to be affected by this change. Think of the video rental store of the 1980s and 1990s. At one time we visited a store with hundreds of movies shelved like a library from which we picked one or two we wanted to watch. We had a week (or so) to view, rewind (in the Video Home System days), and return the video or face a late fee. If a particular movie we wanted to watch was not on the shelf, we had to do without it and hold our hopes up for next week when it may be returned. If our local video rental place was small, or the manager/selector did not agree with our artistic and cultural sensibilities, the selection of movies might not be as varied as we wanted. Then came Netflix. Before long, people were able to access these films in their homes and all but lost the need to visit the video rental shop any longer.

Despite the assumptions of many nonlibrarians, not all library material is available online, so the analogy between science libraries and video rental stores breaks down when we get to special collections and legacy material. But an expanding body of literature is available outside of the institutional library, whether licensed or available on demand via websites, repositories, or by simply emailing the author for a reprint.

A SELF-SERVICE STORY

For much of the last 100 years, the peer-reviewed journal article has been the most widely used vehicle for scientific communication. And until the 1990s, library users who wanted to find articles on a certain subject used

Science Libraries in the Self-Service Age
DOI: https://doi.org/10.1016/B978-0-08-102033-3.00001-5

the printed indexes which were specific to a set of journals in a particular discipline. This method was slow, involving manual lookup of terms in what could end up being dozens of physical volumes. In addition, users had to (again, manually) write down the publication data for articles that interested them. With that list of items to find in the stacks, she had to then refer to the catalog and lookup journal titles, recording library location and call number. Not only slow, this process often involved an initial training session by the librarian since the subject-based indexes were often arranged differently from one another and users needed some guidance. While this and other predigital library services may have had a self-service component, it was not something that library users looked forward to handling themselves.

Among the first bibliographic indexes to move online was Medline, a digital version of the printed, *Index Medicus*, which became available online by the early 1970s. When this and other article indexes were made available in digital form, library users seeking articles could ask the librarian to perform a search on their behalf. This may have been easier for the user if more time-consuming. The librarian performed the search under constraints of time and number of records viewed since online access was commonly billed on a per-minute and per-citation view/print basis. The potential expense of searching these online indexes required that the librarian work closely with the patron in a preliminary interview of the exact needs. Once a search strategy was formulated offline, it could be executed against the database. For reasons of this method of costing, the librarian was the gatekeeper to this data and the service was part of the librarian's duties.

It was not long until science librarians introduced users to self-service bibliographic databases. At first, they were available via CD-ROM, usually on a single workstation, most often in the library and using proprietary software. These were mailed to the librarians with regular supplements. Users could go back to helping themselves, but they still had to visit the library, get the disk from the librarian (sometimes multiple disks as early CD-ROMs had limited storage capacity), and still receive some initial instruction on how to use the database since user interfaces varied and may not have been very intuitive.

By the 1990s, these article indexes became available via the internet, and by that time, most researchers had a personal computer on their desk which was connected to the organization's network. Where the library licensed and provided access to online databases, authentication was often network based so that there was no need to share, store, and remember usernames and passwords. Network-based authentication to these licensed (or in the case of PubMed, freely available) resources meant that users did not have to visit the library or consult a librarian to find articles. Of course they would be doing themselves a favor if they took advantage of database search training sessions which the library offered, but in either case, the user was in full self-service mode.

The scientist could search, view, refine, and select relevant papers to print or download. There was no longer a need to manually write down journal names, volume, and pagination anymore. As library systems evolved to integrate and cooperate with one another, the user could capture the bibliographic data to a reference-management tool whether locally installed on her workstation or web based. And at the click of a button from within the online index, she could search her local library catalog for the journal and/or generate an interlibrary loan request from her library's online request form.

With the introduction of the freely available Google Scholar in 2003, scientists could search for literature wherever they happened to be. While there are always leaders and laggards with any innovation, it is worth noting that scientists found out about this obviously game-changing tool at almost the same time as librarians, and they developed a dexterity in using Google Scholar almost as fast as their librarians did.

The above scenario illustrates the move in research libraries to a self-service model. Countless things that users once relied on librarians to do for them can now be done by themselves (for better or worse). This trend has several implications for science libraries, among them the imperative for flexibility among library staff to investigate and offer new services for their patrons who may no longer need help with certain tasks.

The emergence of Google Scholar is interesting in that it is emblematic of this rapid movement of services out of the librarian's hands and into the user's. Many other new science library services are often developed when a librarian discovers a new website, tool, or other gadget that can help library users in their day-to-day work. S/he investigates the tool and how it might apply to the scientist's work, and s/he uses it to help. The new gadget or web service may become a standard part of the librarian's toolkit, but soon the scientist realizes that he or she can help themselves, especially where no paid account and individual credential are required. Paid services with access controlled for monetary reasons were necessarily librarian mediated, but when available to all on the organizations' network (appearing to be "free"), a self-service model began to emerge. IP-based services which are licensed or free services fall quickly to the self-service model just as happened with searching online indexing and abstracting services. Eventually, the librarian is mostly cut out of the process, and self-service equilibrium is reached once again.

The institutional repository (IR) movement presents another useful illustration. While archiving and the institutional stewardship of an organization's scientific research output is a long-term goal of most IRs, their appeal to many scientists is that it provides a place to easily share and direct inquiries for their electronic reprints. In the early 2000s, repositories began to multiply as many scientific institutions installed and configured platforms to accept and archive digital content. Soon social network services such as ResearchGate and Academia.edu emerged, providing scientists with a much simpler interface than was common among most IR platforms and scientists flocked to them, removing that service from the librarian's control.

In some cases, scholars are beginning to discover these new services themselves even before librarians have time to raise awareness. Figshare is a good example of a service that many scientists seem to have discovered at the same time (or before) their librarian. Librarians who do not discover and use these emerging tools early and teach or inform scientists risk becoming obsolete.

Many online discovery products include advanced search, display, download, and other tools that end users typically ignore (Haglund and Olsson, 2008). But science librarians can exploit some of these features to pilot services that might otherwise be overlooked, for example, with the commercial products, Scopus and Web of Knowledge which allow not only identification of publications on a certain topic but also of institutions and potential collaborators, metrics for publications, and evaluation of research outputs.

However, the advantage will probably be short-lived: these and almost all advanced services will one day be performed directly by users, and therefore, science librarians will need to continually search for innovations of which their user base is yet unaware in order to develop new services and remain relevant to their parent organization. Librarians may one day serve as the means to discover not newly published literature but new tools to foster efficiency in the research enterprise including a wider range of activity that scientists are normally involved with.

Science librarians should keep abreast of popular blogs, news, and Twitter feeds where new services, gadgets, and other items of interest to the science publishing community might appear. This can be overwhelming, but the use of Really Simple Syndication (RSS) formats to syndicate this content provides a more efficient way to cover this content more thoroughly. A proficiency and current awareness of new tools and services can ensure that science librarians are the go-to for latest developments in these areas which may not necessarily in the domain expertise of the scientist.

ADMINISTRATION AND PLANNING FOR NEW SERVICES

Sometimes, service development tends to be spontaneous and limited, while at other times, services are developed more systematically than sporadically and only after an initial inquiry, a definition of the problem, and the creation of a team or effort to solve it. The latter approach has advantages and disadvantages, and it should be noted that it is often a much slower process and can become a victim of mission creep. But this approach also ensures buy-in from management and keeps all parties informed who may ultimately be affected by the development and implementation of a new service.

Among the most basic services science librarians can provide is to inform their users that digital publishing is disrupting not only how users read but how libraries manage and collect published outputs. Scientists may often be lost in their laboratory or field work, but a succinct and clear presentation of the issues and soliciting their thoughts would be doing both librarian and user a great service.

Perhaps the most important service a science librarian can offer grows out of developing a real interest in the research of the library users. When librarians become conversant in the field and take an interest in what the scientists do—particularly their way of documenting and writing/publishing their research—then librarians can most easily create and develop new services (Gibson and Coniglio, 2010).

One could reasonably conclude that having someone else do your work for you is more desirable than doing it yourself. And for something like housework that is probably true. But it has become clear that most research library users like and want to do their research themselves, often from their offices or labs (Tenopir et al., 2012). Science librarians need to consider all implications this brings forth.

REFERENCES

Gibson, C., Coniglio, J.W. 2010. The new liaison librarian: competencies for the 21st century academic librarian. In: Walter, Scott and Williams, Karen, (Eds.), The Expert Library: Staffing, Sustaining and Advancing the Academic Library in the 21st Century, Association of College & Research Libraries, Chicago, pp. 93—126.

Haglund, L., Olsson, P., 2008. The impact on university libraries of changes in information behavior among academic researchers: a multiple case study. J. Academic Librarianship 34 (1), 52—59. Available from: https://doi.org/10.1016/j.acalib.2007.11.010.

Tenopir, C., Volentine, R., King, D.W., 2012. Article and book reading patterns of scholars: findings for publishers. Learned Pub. 25 (4), 279—291. Available from: https://doi.org/10.1087/20120407.

Yeh, S.-T., Walter, Z., 2016. Determinants of service innovation in academic libraries through the lens of disruptive innovation. College Res. Lib. 77 (6), 795—804. Available from: https://doi.org/10.5860/crl.77.6.795.

RESOURCES

Information Today News Breaks

Hanging Together (OCLC Research blog) hangingtogether.org

Scholarly Kitchen

ALA—Schol-Comm Listserv

STM Industry News

KnowledgeSpeak Newsletter and KnowledgeSpeak Blog

LSE (London School of Economics and Political Science Impact Blog)

CHAPTER 2

Introduction: Science Libraries and Service Innovation

The first step in reimagining the academic libraries is to determine the jobs we are being hired to do. As we do so we need to recognize that at the end of the day what we should be about is not saving the library. Rather ... it should be about providing a product or service that can help students and faculty more effectively, conveniently and affordably, do a job they've been trying to do in their scholarly lives. If the library is to provide value, it needs to find those jobs it can do that cannot be done more effectively by others.

Lewis (2016)

The changes that networked technology have brought were anticipated nowhere more eagerly than in libraries. When we first imagined connecting computers seamlessly to electronic books, journals, catalogs and indexes, it seemed as if an ocean of information would be available in digital form and any of us could find out anything we wanted on demand. Many subsequently thought that libraries would be rendered obsolete. And while it is true that libraries have not gone away, librarians have to admit that today some collections and services are used far less than they once were.

Until the 1990s, for example, library users had to engage in personal contact at the library to use most services. Just about the only thing a library user could do for him or herself was find a book in the catalog. Users required personal assistance when searching bibliographic databases, locating and retrieving materials, getting reference help, and borrowing via interlibrary loan. These all required some exchange—by telephone or in person—with a librarian. Today most of these services can be both requested and delivered digitally from outside the library building.

Certainly, the "ready reference" type questions that people once called the public library to answer are no longer necessarily answered by librarians. Questions like, Who was the vice president under Theodore Roosevelt?[1] or In what year did Malaysia gain independence from

---

[1] No vice president during his first term; Charles W. Fairbanks during his second term.

Science Libraries in the Self-Service Age
DOI: https://doi.org/10.1016/B978-0-08-102033-3.00002-7

Britain?,[2] are the questions that we can answer more quickly ourselves than by calling or visiting a library as we may have done in the past.

As for collections, take a moment to think of all the books that once occupied the reference area but that have been replaced by search engines and other web resources. Many mainstream dictionaries and thesauruses, road atlases, telephone directories, almanacs, encyclopedias, and other books on the reference shelves are not consulted nearly as much today since anyone with an internet connection can find for him/herself the information that was once exclusive to these printed materials. Despite this automation; the connectedness of a vast majority of the world; and the emergence of things like Google Scholar, Google Books, and many other trappings of the Internet, we still have libraries and librarians. However, current trends indicate that it will become necessary for libraries to develop new services to remain relevant to their parent institution.

BUSINESS AND SELF-SERVICE

To the general public, it is in the business world where the effects of the Internet are most easily recognizable. Facing ever-increasing cost pressures, business have tried to reduce expenses by enticing customers to help themselves, often using the Internet to push many day-to-day activities toward a self-service model. It happened, for example, with retail and banking and government services, as users of these services often no longer require interpersonal contact to transact most business. Instead, people can now take care of many routine services themselves online as they do their shopping, pay their taxes, renew their automobile registration, or a host of other activities which once required an in-person transaction.

In addition to traditional retail transactions, communication media has also gone digital. At one time, we physically handled movies, music, newspapers, and magazines, often visiting a store or library and buying, renting, or borrowing the item to bring home. Today much of our popular media is streamed online. And while electronic books may not yet be widely adopted due to a number of factors, clearly the current trends in retrieval and consumption of entertainment and other media follows the online self-service model we see with other organizations.

---

[2] 1957.

APPLICATION TO LIBRARIES

Research libraries may not be subject to the same forces or to the same degree as companies in the private sector, but because *all* organizations are interested in controlling costs and making operations more efficient, it is inevitable that libraries in some ways mimic trends we see in the business world (Mullins et al., 2007). Whether or not libraries wholeheartedly embrace this way of service transaction, it is clear that users of science libraries are keen to adopt at least to some degree the self-service model we have seen develop in other parts of our lives.

This is exemplified by the migration of scientists to adopt electronic journals (perhaps after some initial reluctance). Primarily because of the publication practices and formats in the sciences, self-service literature retrieval is most pronounced in science libraries. In most disciplines, articles are the common currency of scientific communication. The peer-reviewed scientific paper tends to be 10 pages or less in length (varying by subdiscipline) which lends itself to digital delivery and sharing in a way that longer form publications do not.

No longer is it necessary to visit the library and pull a journal volume to photocopy an article since a growing body of this literature is available online not only from the publisher but in repositories and other sources. The easy distribution of papers as PDF files has led to informal networks of sharing reprints among scientists. The inclusion of email addresses in journal articles ensures that if all else fails, a reader can easily contact one of the coauthors and request a reply with the article attached if available.

REDUCED LIBRARY VISITS

This increasing availability of digital versions of scientific papers and the consequent reduction in library visits may ultimately diminish the visibility of science libraries. It is clear that scientists' visits to their research library have been sharply reduced in the digital era (The Advisory Board Company, 2011). Many scientists still embrace the nostalgia of perusing the library stacks as reminiscent of their own days in the university, but today time is too tight for this luxury (Flaxbart, 2001; Haines et al., 2010). The trend toward consolidation of science libraries within university library systems is a clear recognition of the reduction of in-person visits (Zdravkovska, 2011). Despite efforts by librarians to publicize the indexes and other resources which they license, many scientists find articles themselves online via Google Scholar and other web searches (although they may not realize the content is available to them only because they are on the campus network where access has been arranged by the library).

USER GROUPS

The "help-yourself" style of online library usage and the corresponding decline in library visits means that in order to survive organizationally, librarians have had to develop not only new services for existing users but also for new user groups. New service creation often requires identifying new audiences and their needs. These user groups can be individuals who have typically not visited or come in contact with the library for research purposes in the past but can also include the traditional users who have needs beyond literature retrieval that libraries may be in a position to serve. In both cases, new activities and processes must be established, or else science libraries may become little more than legacy print storage, content licensing, and interlibrary loan operations.

SAME USERS

Researchers have traditionally used the library to collect references and reading material to support a larger cycle of research activity which includes grant writing, field and lab work, and communicating their findings. But today, science library users are being served in ways which go beyond collection development and access to purchased or licensed resources. It is becoming more obvious to science librarians that the same people who have used the libraries for years to find reading material have now emerged as a new user community based on different needs. While the recipient of support is a familiar face to the science library staff, in that sense, they represent a "new" audience. Service to this community is one of the foundations of recent innovation in science library services (Kronman and Lundén, 2013).

Hence, science librarians are beginning to identify different stages of the research life cycle where they can inject new services and renew the library's status as a service provider. Services like data-management consultation; open-access advocacy; guidance on compliance with public-access mandates; and digitizing, enhancing, and publicizing research outcomes are activities that science librarians have moved into given new emphases in research organizations. The open-access movement in particular has spawned a suite of services that target the traditional library user in new ways. In order to provide these new services, many science librarians are recognizing the new usage patterns of the library and taking advantage of time no longer spent on traditional activities which had been dependent on in-person visits by patrons. The development of these nontraditional services ensures that science librarians continue to provide value to the organization where their roles may have otherwise been eroded.

A simple example of a service which may have become obsolete in science libraries recently is the daily display and rotation of new journal issues. The routine may be familiar to science librarians as a long standing part of journal-issue processing, but it is a mostly outdated method of keeping abreast of current literature in the digital era. Many scientists have discovered and helped themselves to table of contents and alerts services online or via email which eliminates the need to browse the daily display. This means that librarians no longer need to sort incoming journal issues by date of receipt, track how long they should be displayed, and then manually shelve them with the bound issues on the shelves. This service is no longer essential and used less and less by scientists today (Flaxbart, 2001). And in fact, many science libraries today have either canceled the print version or canceled altogether many subscriptions due to budget pressures such that the journal issues available for display are fewer in most libraries. The time saved from discontinuing this handling of physical issues (and other traditional but little used services) is likely better spent on new activities designed to support other segments of the research process.

NEW USERS

The emergence of nontraditional library activity parallels to many businesses over the years which have had to move into a different product line in order to remain relevant (Mullen, 2010, p. 138). Successful businesses tend to move into the most profitable product or service line, regardless of their original mission. For example, Apple, IBM, General Electric, and many other companies at one time or another have successfully moved to a new product over the years (Sanburn, 2011), presumably because the return on investment was greater in a new service or product area. And while librarians may not be motivated by profits, high usage is in a sense an adequate proxy for profits. In any event, science librarians cannot ignore the need to cultivate different user groups at their institutions (Feltes et al., 2012) since the original user group—the reader—increasingly has his/her demands satisfied without the need for interpersonal contact with a librarian.

These new user groups are found in organizational units at research institutions that typically do not visit the library, or if they do, they may only be looking for a quiet place to get away. Staff outside of research units may not yet realize what librarians can do for them. These include offices of public affairs, social media, higher administration, IT/webmasters, sponsored research and advancement, and fundraising, to name a few. Librarians possess the skills and knowledge to help these groups perform their functions better in ways that may not be apparent to either librarian or these new constituents since these groups' service needs are not typically met by scientific and technical reading material.

For example, a collection of information about research being conducted at the institution can be a valuable resource for these underserved offices. Compiling research publication metadata (an institutional or faculty bibliography) representing scholarship produced at the institution is one valuable resource that can be leveraged for many subsequent services. This data can be reused for academic computing, the creation of dynamic website content, public information offices, social media, or fundraising groups to inform them of current research. Many science libraries are moving into expanded researcher profiling services which collect a complete picture of the work of the scholars who are affiliated with the organization. This is equally useful for those mentioned earlier who need to keep abreast of current research at the organization.

The recognition of these new audiences is evident in the products and services recently offered by library vendors. Many represent a movement away from traditional abstracting and indexing service and into research evaluation tools marketed directly to university administration. Likewise, publishers have responded to the open access (OA) movement and other changes by acknowledging the need for new audiences or offering new services to existing audiences. Many of them have launched new or have enhanced existing services such as researcher identification and profiling systems, institutional aggregation of data for metrics and evaluation and others outside the services for which they have been well-known for years (Dempsey, 2014). The possibilities to serve users outside the traditional scientist group vary by institution, but the bottom line is that the return on investment of providing literature to which users can increasingly help themselves is diminishing.

COST SAVINGS AS A SERVICE

In addition to developing new services and/or finding new audiences, a highly valued activity in any organization is providing an existing service at a lower cost. This should not be overlooked when science librarians think about creating value for an organization. Doing things with fewer resources often goes unnoticed by the direct recipient of the service but is aimed at upper administration of an organization who always appreciate conserving scarce resources—the most scarce being money and space (we have already seen how libraries save time, another scarce resource). Holding down costs inevitably improves services as far as the institutional management is concerned and librarians can consider delivering service more efficiently as a service to the institution as a whole (Courant, 2008).

The move toward access rather than ownership is yet another trend from the business world which is influencing library work. Just as the rise of the "sharing economy" emphasizes access rather than ownership of goods (Eckhardt and Bardhi, 2015), libraries are now providing access to content rather than purchasing it outright. Licensing electronic content is one of the new processes that librarians have had to learn in the digital era. In this sense, libraries and publishers have moved from product to service. One might draw a comparison to the US economy as a whole, which has moved away from manufacturing and toward services. American Library Association past president, Feldman (2015), may have put it best, "the future relevance of libraries and library professionals will depend on what we *do* for people rather than what we *have* for people" [emphasis mine].

Another service in the realm of resource saving comes in the form of consolidation of print collections. Moving print materials to an off-site storage facility with perhaps a scan-on-demand component frees up space on campus which organizations' administration will appreciate. The off-site storage of legacy print collections and consortial arrangements with like institutions to share print storage and/or cooperatively collect print collections can save space on the central campus, and this is a very valuable resource for the institution as a whole (Lynn et al., 2011). Given the reduction in personal visits to the library, the newfound space can be used for different purposes by the libraries or the institution.

The examples showing the different service models are intentionally drawn to show a parallel to the business world. This may be objectionable to librarians who work in academic institutions, but this will inevitably change. As a 2007 ACRL report declares, "Students will increasingly view themselves as customers and consumers, expecting high-quality facilities and services" (Mullins et al., 2007). We can safely substitute "researchers" or "scientists" for the term "students." The use of business terms is intentional if somewhat unpalatable to a profession rooted in public service and education. However, any research library director today knows that costs must be controlled and services shifted in response to a changing funding landscape.

SHIFTING PRIORITIES

All the new services mentioned here are possible only after scientists' need or interest in existing services wane and the service is discontinued (see displaying current journals above). Freeing up staff time is necessary to provide more targeted support to scientists with new services, and it will require reevaluating activities which do not have a high return on the investment of time. In addition, support from library leadership for reprioritization of activities and resources (both monetary and human) are essential for new service sustainability over time (Vinopal and McCormick, 2013).

It is common for scientists to react to new services of this kind with skepticism and reluctance. This may be due to their traditional perception of librarians and their duties and association with print materials' collecting. While some scientists feel overwhelmed by administrative demands of research and publishing and may likewise be slow to adopt digital technologies to ease these new burdens, many still feel that librarians do not understand and have no place in their research workflow. Development and adoption of new services can therefore be slow. The best approach to implementation will vary by institution, but sometimes, informal conversation and information gathering are helpful as is a stealth launch or pilot to test receptivity of users.

A worthwhile strategy in many cases is to work with incoming graduate or postdoctoral students. Being digital natives and in the early part of their career, these people are often very receptive and eager to consider working with the library in new ways. Typically, postdocs and graduate students are younger and more open to technological solutions to research problems. They also generally are the ones on whom the administration of research activity will fall anyway, including data collection, transcription, writing manuscripts, and other manual tasks. They have the ear of senior scientists and perhaps their trust at least with regard to activities not traditionally associated with library staff. These younger scholars are hungry for any opportunity to advance their careers and are consequently open to innovation and anything that may distinguish them in the eyes of senior scientists who enjoy some degree of exemption from these new ways of managing and producing research.

BIOMEDICAL ROOTS

Many innovative library services and tools began in the biomedical area and spread to other life sciences. This is undoubtedly due to the head start that biomedical and hospital libraries have enjoyed thanks to the work done at the National Library of Medicine. Certainly, Medline/PubMed is widely regarded as the granddaddy of online bibliographic databases as is evidenced by the widespread adoption of the PubMed Identifier. Probably because medical research had the most practical application and broad appeal (healthcare improvement), the resources were made available to index and unify the biomedical literature before many other indexing and abstracting services were available. Another strong indication of the NLM's leadership position in providing the platform for service development is the widespread adoption of the Journal Article Tagging Suite, a NISO standard for publishing scientific literature online that began at the NLM and the PubMed Central repository. In addition, the fact that both VIVO and Profiles RNS research information management systems were originally funded by NIH attests to the well-developed informatics and research infrastructure in the biomedical sciences.

It may be helpful to think of the NLM impact on scientific literature as analogous to the Library of Congress' impact on cataloging monographs. Science librarians who follow service innovation can thank the early investment in the NLM for creating standards and platforms which have enabled many of the self-service components of library use today.

MEDIATE AUTOMATED SERVICES—AT FIRST

One pattern that seems to be repeated in research libraries is the intermediate adoption of online tools and services by librarians on behalf of patrons. Rather than train patrons on how to set up services (alerts, searches, etc.), it is often more fruitful for the librarian to do so on behalf of the scientist and forward results to him/her. Scientists, especially those with established labs and careers, are busy and often understandably reluctant to engage with new features and innovations, that is, until the librarian proves its value. If the service provides value, often the scientists who were too busy to investigate initially often help themselves and create their own accounts, subscriptions, or otherwise engages the service directly.

ABOUT THIS BOOK

This book is intended for science librarians and others who work in research libraries and who are beginning to recognize that the world of digital storage and delivery of publications has changed the way that our physical spaces are used. Librarians who may not have yet had the opportunity to plan and develop new services but who are ready to respond to the research needs of scientists beyond developing and managing collections and providing reference are the primary audience of this book. Librarians who may understand that their skills are most cost effective in collecting, curating, and exposing research materials created by their institution's scientists rather than externally published material but who have not begun to implement some of the ideas they have developed should find this book a good place to begin if nothing else.

Finally, a note about the speed of change in the digital world. This book illustrates the variety of new, nontraditional services being tested and offered in science libraries today. Because information technology moves quickly, it may turn out that the ideas and suggestions for new services in science libraries will become obsolete just as quickly. Many of the tools described here which are used in implementing new services may soon be obsolete, acquired by other companies, rebranded, etc. For that reason, the recommendations in this book are mentioned here only as examples.

But the idea remains the same: needs of science library users are changing, and increasingly, scientists are able to meet their own needs for finding or retrieving research publications. This is an activity that librarians—while not abandoning completely—can safely cede to their users. This concession, while it may appear to undermine the usefulness of having a librarian, will actually allow them to create and implement services that fill long standing research support needs in the organization.

Scientists' library needs will continue to change as long as models for publishing and scientific communication evolve. In order to meet these new needs, science librarians will have to keep current on new tools and services, explore their feasibility for supporting library services, and adopt or abandon them as quickly as they emerge. Some of the implications may violate the foundations of what many of us were taught while earning a traditional degree in library science, but it is a reality we need to confront in order to survive professionally.

REFERENCES

The Advisory Board Company, 2011. Redefining the Academic Library: Managing the Migration to Digital Information Services. The Advisory Board Company, Washington, DC.

Courant, P.N., 2008. The future of the library in the research university. In No Brief Candle: Reconceiving Research Libraries for the 21st Century. Council on Library and Information Resources, Washington, DC, pp. 21–27.

Dempsey, L., 2014. Research Information Management Systems—A New Service Category?—Lorcan Dempsey's Weblog. Retrieved November 11, 2015, from <http://orweblog.oclc.org/archives/002218.html>.

Eckhardt, G.M., Bardhi, F., 2015. The Sharing Economy Isn't About Sharing at All. Harvard Business Review, https://hbr.org/2015/01/the-sharing-economy-isnt-about-sharing-at-all.

Feldman, S., 2015. The future of the MLIS: imparting enduring values with changing instruction models. Am. Lib. 46 (11/12), 5.

Feltes, C., Gibson, S., Miller, H., 2012. Envisioning the Future of Science Libraries at Academic Research Institutions. Retrieved from: <https://darchive.mblwhoilibrary.org/bitstream/handle/1912/5653/Banbury_Envisioning_Future_Research_Libraries_12202012.pdf>.

Flaxbart, D., 2001. Conversations with chemists. Sci. Technol. Lib. 21 (3–4), 5–26. Available from: http://doi.org/10.1300/J122v21n03_02.

Haines, L.L., Light, J., O'Malley, D., Delwiche, F.A., 2010. Information-seeking behavior of basic science researchers: implications for library services. J. Med. Lib. Assoc. 98 (1), 73–81.

Kronman, U., Lundén, A., 2013. Can open access create a sound scholarly publishing market? ScieCom Info 9 (2), http://journals.lub.lu.se/index.php/sciecominfo/article/view/7298.

Lewis, D.W., 2016. Reimagining the Academic Library. Rowman & Littlefield, Lanham, MD.

Lynn, V.A., FitzSimmons, M., Robinson, C.K., 2011. Special report: symposium on transformational change in health sciences libraries: space, collections, and roles. J.

Med. Lib. Assoc. 99 (1), 82–87. Available from: http://doi.org/10.3163/1536-5050.99.1.014.

Mullen, L.B., 2010. Open Access and Its Practical Impact on the Work of Academic Librarians: Collection Development, Public Services, and the Library and Information Science Literature. Chandos Pub, Oxford. Available from: http://doi.org/10.1016/B978-1-84334-593-0.50003-4.

Mullins, J.L., Allen, F.R., Hufford, J.R., 2007. Top ten assumptions for the future of academic libraries and librarians: a report from the ACRL research committee, Association of College and Research Libraries (ACRL). C&RL News 68 (4), 240–246.

Sanburn, J., 2011. Ten Companies that Radically Transformed their Businesses. *Time*.

Vinopal, J., McCormick, M., 2013. Supporting digital scholarship in research libraries: scalability and sustainability. J. Lib. Adm. 53 (1), 27–42. Available from: http://doi.org/10.1080/01930826.2013.756689.

Zdravkovska, N., 2011. Most common subject branch libraries. In Academic Branch Libraries in Changing Times. Chandos Publishing, Amsterdam, pp. 65–90.

PART I

Non Traditional Library Services

CHAPTER 3

Scholarly Communication Services

... publishers are investing in author services more and more, as scholarly communication is becoming increasingly about providing services to those who create the content to help them maximise their impact, and the library is mirroring what's happening in the publishing industry in terms of increasing author services, and being a much more author-centric environment.

Jones (2016)

EMERGENCE OF SCHOLARLY COMMUNICATION SERVICES

The first and perhaps easiest step to take outside of the conventional library roles of book buying, preserving, and/or reference support are services that deal with research produced within the scientific organization. In recent years, research libraries have seen the creation of a set of services (and in some cases, position titles and library departments) most commonly called "scholarly communication" services. This can include a variety of activities in support of researchers, but one common thread is that these services approach the scientists not as a reader of library-acquired materials but rather as a creator of scholarly works. Scholarly communication services today can include a wide variety of activities including support for publishing activities and/or creation of descriptive metadata representing research done at the parent organization. This is an important concept in science libraries today since the self-service nature of library use has reduced reader dependence on librarians who must therefore search for additional ways to remain relevant to their organization (Niu et al., 2010; Jubb, 2016).

Scholarly communication services were born primarily in response to the "serials crisis" which was first described in the 1980s. Unsustainable increases in journal subscription costs over the past 30 years, particularly in the sciences, have resulted in routine cancellations and a potential crisis in library collection development. There are several explanations offered for this runaway inflation (which in some cases exceeded even the annual

Science Libraries in the Self-Service Age
DOI: https://doi.org/10.1016/B978-0-08-102033-3.00003-9

inflation of health-care costs) which are outside the scope of this book. But one thing is clear: when there is a third-party paying for journal subscriptions, neither the producer (publisher) nor the consumer (reader/scientist) seems to have an incentive to negotiate a better price. The library as subscriber occupies the role as third-party payer. Readers of scientific articles have been largely unaware of the dollar cost of most library subscriptions and have come to expect journals to be renewed annually without interruption. Scientific publishers have consequently enjoyed a customer base where purchasing decisions were almost always continued indefinitely.

SCIENTIST AS AUTHOR

Because scientists as readers have largely begun to help themselves to peer-reviewed literature, forward thinking science librarians now treat their core user community as both readers and writers. That is, the traditional library users are also creators of the scholarly literature which research libraries spend so much on collecting. The following scenario illustrates the scientist's role as author of scientific literature. When budget pressure compels science librarians to review current subscriptions, they frequently invite readers to participate. This serials cancellation exercise is a near-annual event in academic libraries due to incessant inflation among subscriptions and flat library acquisitions budgets. During these solicitations by librarians for input from scientists, a comment that sometimes comes up from those who oppose cancellation of a particular title goes something like, "You can't cancel *The Journal of XXX*. I publish there!" This may come as a surprise to many science librarians who have been trained in traditional collection development and who feel that their job is to build collections and subscribe to journals on behalf of readership and research. The expenditure of acquisitions funds for the purpose of ensuring financial sustainability of journals so that their constituent scientists can count on a vehicle in which to publish their research is not the way librarians have been trained to think. But this example shows that in addition to readers, a significant segment of journal publishers' market is the scholar-as-author (Kronman and Lundén, 2013). The awareness of this additional role for scientists is something that science librarians must recognize and adapt to or risk losing the attention and support of their core community.

NEW AUDIENCE

Because scientists participate and contribute to the process of publishing research and because they are not paid as authors, reviewers, or editors, the conventional wisdom is that research organizations have essentially given away content freely and then bought it back at prices that have increased unsustainably. The difficulty (some would say impossibility) of renewing science journals indefinitely and the consequent new ways of thinking about and acquiring peer-reviewed literature at some institutions has resulted in a change in service emphasis.

Journal literature is consumed one article at a time, and because of their increasing availability in the digital age, scientific articles are seen more and more as discrete units, separate from the parent journal. The disintermediation of journal content has led to the rise of so-called mega-journals of which PLoS ONE is among the earliest successful examples. The conceptual and physical separation of articles from the journal in which they appear has also led to things like repositories where reprints from an organization's researchers can be collected but provide no common subject thread or unification that a journal title does aside from the institution where the work was done. Journal disintermediation in the digital age means that articles once associated with other papers in the same volume or issue of a journal are now recognized as lacking any formal connection. In the same way that certain discipline-specific journals can nonetheless include articles on a wide variety of subtopics with very narrow readership and appeal, repositories and preprint servers collect papers which likely have an audience that is exclusive and largely unconcerned with any of the other electronic reprints held there.

Some see this "disintermediation" of journal content as leading research libraries to reconsider their primary role from purchasing/licensing externally published material to one of capturing and exposing an institution's internal research (Dempsey et al., 2014). The seemingly narrow reader market for each individual article has led to a reevaluation of services in science libraries.

RISE OF REPOSITORIES

One of the earliest scholarly communication services to emerge in science libraries is the creation and management of a repository of reprints for dissemination of the organization's research. This was largely a response to the serials crisis as it was felt that an organization is entitled to capture the fruits of its own research rather than giving it away and buying it back from publishers in the form of subscriptions. In addition to peer-reviewed literature, some repositories host locally produced materials or digitized texts, but the original intent of many repositories was to collect, describe, and archive the research output of an institution including content which might one day be available only by subscription.

However, it turned out that relying on authors to submit publications to an institutional repository (IR) left many repositories near empty save for locally produced and unpublished material. Scientists may largely agree in principle with the reasons for a repository but most are too busy to contribute their reprints. Hence, the most successful IR content recruitment has come through some sort of library-mediated deposit where the library staff takes an active role in the identification, description, and ingest of the organization's published research.

But even where the acquisition of digital materials is not possible, the collection of metadata describing the publications—as long as it is done institution-wide—can be almost as valuable to the research organization as the collection of associated reprints. A database of publications (often called a "faculty bibliography" at universities) appeals to many audiences at a scientific research organization, but its utility increases dramatically if it includes all scientists in all departments. This may be difficult to achieve for several reasons, but the ability to represent the research of a given organization by its published works depends on being as comprehensive as possible.

The collection of metadata for published output begins with the systematic identification of publications authored by scientists who work at the home institution. This is a basic service both to the individual scientists but also the institution in many ways as it can be leveraged for different purposes and audiences, showcasing the output of the organization and potentially setting up other services (Sterman and Clark, 2017). This service has its roots in health science and large hospital libraries, probably owing to the exhaustive coverage, free availability, and associated services built on top of the PubMed database.

Because most scientific publishers include a statement of author affiliation somewhere in the body of the paper, and because some bibliographic services parse the author address/affiliation and make it searchable, a series of stored searches and alerts can be created to systematically collect publication data by an organization's authors. At this time, services such as

PubMed, Google Scholar (GS), HighWire Press, BioOne, and many commercial and nonprofit publishers permit saved searches with email alert capabilities.

However, variability in the listed form of the name of the organization means that these searches may miss some of an institution's publications. And although many science journals have made the transition to online publishing, there are still many journals that are not indexed or their articles are otherwise not discoverable via standard search tools. For this reason, the strategy of searching on an institution name and creating alerts may not be a complete picture of an organization's research. In addition, some indexes do not offer searching restricted to author address, and searches done against the full text of articles are bound to return false hits among the results (e.g., where an organization's name is mentioned in the body of an article or the acknowledgment section, but authored by scientists without any affiliation). It is worth noting that there are commercial services which aggregate an institution's publication data using basically the same methods, but because they use software which is professionally developed, the results are likely more accurate and easily refined.

STANDARD IDENTIFIERS

The practice of collecting metadata about research outputs is made much easier by the use of unique identifiers. Not only the use of digital object identifiers (DOIs) as items on which to match or to use in web services such as social media metrics, but the institution-wide implementation of Open Researcher and Contributor ID (ORCIDs) for all scholars enables easy sharing of data related to researchers affiliated with the organization. It is hoped that with widespread adoption of author identifiers such as ORCID by both publishers and scientists could make the identification of a research organization's published output a near-completely automated process.

The systematic search of online literature for papers authored by an institution's scientists boosts the success of this kind of service because, as with repository content, it is clear that most scientists have shown a reluctance to engage in the manual upkeep of their publication lists outside of maintaining a curriculum vitae (Salo, 2008). However, for the publications that are not online or easily findable that way, the creation of a simple web form provides a method to collect these overlooked items, and where representation in the database is low, may be welcome by at least a few authors or their designees. An organization's webmaster can set up the form to save the data in a format specified by the librarian or collecting office for ease of import or integration into the bibliographic data which has been auto-captured.

However, despite these caveats, once a certain level of coverage is reached, the collection of this metadata can gain institution-wide notice and momentum. Something of a network effect may become evident where institutional scientists want their publications in this library-run database because the other authors at the organization are represented there.

COPY CATALOGING

Some science librarians may choose to store the bibliographic data directly in their repository platform from the beginning, while others may use a separate application to manage the metadata. There are advantages and disadvantages to each workflow, and the science librarian can determine which method of content ingest is best for their situation. In the event they are managed separately, the records can be formatted for import to an IR. Most commonly used repository platforms allow the import of metadata whether by delimited format or those used by standard reference management software tools.

The bulk upload of metadata to the IR means that the digital texts need only be matched with existing records in the repository. This becomes a kind of copy cataloging which is of course a longstanding practice in libraries. This method allows staff to avoid the reproduction or re-keying of the metadata (which inevitably includes errors). Liaison librarians, if available, can work with individual scientists/departments to collect their electronic reprints and upload content for their specific users. This has the added effect of fostering the familiarity and integration of the subject librarian with the scientists' work.

It may not be possible to collect electronic texts which correspond to all metadata collected for an institution's publications. It may therefore be possible to export selected records from the publications' database to the IR based on the availability of an electronic reprint.

Some today question the need for repositories as they were originally intended (Coalition for Networked Information, 2017). Informal article sharing and other services such as ResearchGate have contributed to an informal network of reprint sharing, fulfilling the original intent of many repositories. While it is true that the sustainability of some institutional repositories may be legitimately questioned, science librarians should remember and perhaps remind scientists that the long-term prospects of IRs are more transparent than that of a third-party service with no fees yet a funding model that is not clear.

LEVERAGING DATA FOR NEW AUDIENCES

The scholar-as-author in a sense represents a new user community. Although it may be the same person who comes to the library to pick up printed literature or for instruction, the scientist who has his/her publications listed in the library-managed institutional bibliography has a different role as library service user. But it is not only the individual scientist who benefits from library-provided scholarly communication services. The collection, exposure, measurement, and subsequent analysis of research outputs raises the organization's profile and strengthens both the scientific outreach and the capacity for research evaluation by the institution.

Export to an IR is one commonly used case, but there are others. Once a critical mass of bibliographic metadata has been collected, it can be stored centrally or shared with other systems to enable reuse by other units. The data can be exported to a server managed by the IT department or on library-owned hardware. The software or storage format is not important as long as it is made available for use and reuse by other entities on campus. This not only leverages effort for multiple goals, but central storage and management of this data is probably a good practice for its long-term preservation.

The centralized collection and exposure of this data can provide a service to many others in the research organization. Webmasters are particularly keen to reuse bibliographic data on individual scientists' web pages as it relieves them from the task of continually editing pages when new publications are issued. Scientists also benefit from this reuse of the data because it means they no longer have to remind their webmaster or web editor to add their latest publications. In fact, with the collection of this information via automatic alerts, many scientists don't realize their papers have been published until it appears on his/her web page or the librarian sends a report to the department or university leadership.

Where webmasters recognize the benefits of this creation of meaningful content (publication data) and reduced need for their intervention, it may be reasonable to ask for further support for the program. For example, the creation of web applications that query or import publication data in real-time (or near real-time) and allow edits is an area worth exploring as it may allow be an effective method of automating the work of metadata collection and distributing the review and editing to a larger body of staff. Several bibliographic services have application programming interfaces (APIs) that allow systematic query and capture of relevant publication data.

Once the metadata is redisplayed on scientists' web pages, authors may be more compliant in forwarding their reprints to the repository manager. With the inclusion of links to the full text in the repository, the redisplay of metadata becomes much more useful to scientist since external requests for their reprints can be answered by sending a link to the scientist's web page where the requestor can help him or herself. For the author this is often more desirable than looking for a copy of a PDF on his/her hard disk or keeping their ResearchGate account up to date.

Displaying the data on web pages or the IR can be much more effective if certain formats and standards are used. GS has listed best methods to ensure that publication data is included in their search results and most would agree on the value of adopting this—especially the scientists who would like their work discovered on GS. Working with Webmasters to include formats such as RDFa (Resource Description Framework in Attributes) and/or COinS (Context in Span) means that publications are immensely more discoverable and/or usable by persons outside the organization. Among other things, it allows users of reference management software such as Zotero to easily capture publication metadata to their reference list.

But there are people besides scientists who are interested in this data. Public-information offices, communications, and social media people at a research organization are always interested in learning about research conducted at the organization but unfortunately are often unaware of these activities. Likewise, advancement and fundraising offices that often need to market the organization to external donors are happy for stories which can be crafted out of research being conducted. Regular reports to these offices are yet another way to leverage the publication collection with little additional effort.

LOCALLY PRODUCED CONTENT

IR services often include the republication of material which either has not formally been published, was issued in the print era, and/or has some previously unrecognized scholarly value. Some would argue that it is this locally produced and sometimes esoteric content that is most valuable to repositories because it is unavailable elsewhere, and that institutional repositories might be better directed to emphasize this type of material over professionally published articles (Kennison et al., 2013). This material, whether a conference held at the organization or having some other institutional sponsorship, can then be described, exposed via the repository, indexed by standard search engines, and integrated into popular search services such as GS, federated search tools, or other discovery services licensed by the library. In addition, implementing DOIs for this (and other) material published by the organization can further solidify its findability and usability.

DOI CREATION AND MANAGEMENT

Increasingly, publishers ask scientists to share data which supports a manuscript under review and to include a link to the data. This allows readers and perhaps reviewers of the paper to refer to the data themselves. And because publishers recognize the value of the DOI, this is the preferred method of linking. That leaves scientists scrambling to get their figures or tables on a public-facing website and get a DOI for it, often with short notice since the timely issue of their article depends on doing this. Some publishers offer to host this material on their web platform, but where that is not possible, a link to the local (repository) copy of a publication-level dataset is a service that science librarians can provide. Repository managers and science librarians can be a big help here if they are members of a DOI registration agency (such as DataCite). They can ingest the content into the repository with minimal metadata and create a DOI which the scientist/author can send to their editor for inclusion in the paper.

It is also worth mentioning that increasingly research data is itself being considered a publication which is cited by others. The emergence of data citation indexes and metrics along with efforts to standardize the way data is cited both open up possibilities for new services and a support role by science librarians. Both CrossRef (papers) and DataCite (datasets) have open APIs that can be searched, and although descriptive metadata is not consistent, the organization's keywords (or perhaps a list of author ORCIDs from an institution) can yield fruitful results to be collected.

OPEN ACCESS AND ADVOCACY

In addition to the creation of institutional repositories, another response to the serials crisis has been the open-access (OA) movement. This has spawned a set of library services which likewise treats the scientist as author rather than reader. There have been volumes written about OA; therefore, this section will only specify a few examples of services which have been implemented in science libraries.

Scientists have begun to recognize the inevitability of OA in their journal submission choices and the mechanics of how the Gold version of OA works (Laakso et al., 2011). In this model, authors or their support organizations pay an article-processing charge (APC) to cover the costs of publishing. Even though it may be published by a for-profit publisher, the final paper is freely available to read online (however, license terms for reuse can vary). Although funding agencies and other organizations which require OA are making it easier for authors to comply, there is still a role for liaison librarians at several points in the process. A simple recognition of scientists' publishing habits and options can go a long way to cultivating support for these new library services.

For example, an awareness of funder requirements and journal policies, the automatic deposit by journals in PubMed Central (or other repositories), and the ingest of manuscripts into the IR are several possibilities for science librarians to inject themselves into the process. In addition, some scientists may not be aware of practices such as including a line in a grant funding applications to cover the APC or of advocacy for the creation of a fund at their organization to pay APCs.

OPEN-ACCESS MANDATE COMPLIANCE

Because a large part of scientific research is funded by federal grants, many researchers are faced with complying with federal agency procedures on making research outputs available to the public. Even in straightforward situations, this can be burdensome but can be even more tricky if, for example, funding for a specific project draws on federal grants from multiple agencies. Collecting data on funding from the office of sponsored research (or similar office) and/or using online tools to identify funding awards to an organization, a science librarian can begin to associate publications with a particular funder or a specific grant. This not only may assist with compliance with OA mandates but at the same time provides reports to management on results of external support.

It may also be helpful for librarians to inform affected parties of the costs of compliance with OA requirements. Tracking, verification, and reporting of OA materials in response to funding or institutional mandates require some staff and administrative resources that are currently devoted to other activities. Articulating these issues can help to win support from over-burdened scientists and clarify to organizational management that open science—at least as it is practiced currently—has costs that were not previously realized. Science librarians should also anticipate a response that compliance activity should be moved to the library staff.

The choices which are available regarding where to publish their papers, how to comply with OA requirements, and other issues may be viewed by scientists as yet another distraction from their day-to-day work (Mullen, 2010, p. 136). However, scholarly communications librarians who keep informed of these issues are able to offer advice to scientists and/or set up workflows and tools to facilitate compliance. Advising authors on their rights, licensing, and terms of use is admittedly something that is best done by an attorney. However, librarians can offer referral and guidance on the issues where scientists are unfamiliar or unaware of the possibilities and ramifications of the agreements they routinely sign from publishers. In addition, boilerplate language on the web (commonly called "author addenda") suitable for inclusion in many copyright transfer agreements which authors receive from publishers is freely available online (Hirtle, 2006).

Some organizations have standardized the review and approval of author-publication agreements while at others the authors sign on their own behalf or—absent any paperwork—there is some vague but implicit transfer of rights. Science librarians can at least inform all parties of resources which raise awareness of these issues. An example of this is the Sherpa/Romeo website which lists publisher/journal policies on terms of use for articles. On this site, the user can search for journals or publishers to see the standard reuse terms that exist for accepted articles. Users can also download a list of all journals listed on the site with their restrictions or use the API to query for a specific journal if there is a manuscript submission or approval system in place at the institution. In this way, the rights could be automatically captured and displayed at the time of submission to or acceptance by a journal, allowing the librarian or the author to decide on any repository copies or actions to be taken.

ARTICLE-PROCESSING CHARGE MANAGEMENT

While there has been some debate about its value and effectiveness, the management of APCs by a central office is another service in the area of scholarly communications that librarians are at least willing to test. With multiple scientists, publishing in OA journals (often for the same publisher) and paying the APCs, there may be some savings and reduced overhead if these transactions are handled and tracked centrally. An accounting of APCs allows the organization to identify papers that are largely free of copyright restrictions, demonstrate their commitment to OA, and remove an administrative burden from scientists or their staff. Libraries, because they deal with publishers and subscription aggregators regularly, may be a likely candidate for managing this activity. Although it does not yet seem to be as uniform a process as journal subscription management, it is reasonable that one day follow the same model and perhaps be managed by traditional library subscription agents.

However, there are several caveats to keep in mind when considering this kind of service. Among them are whether there is an OA fund to which scholar/authors must apply or a blanket approval for certain journals or publishers. If there are more applicants for the fund than available funding, "How is the money allocated?" "Is there a cap on APCs and if so, who decides where to set the limit?" "How about splitting fees with coauthors in other institutions?" (Sinn et al, 2017). The Scholarly Publishing and Academic Resources Coalition (SPARC) (2007) has created a rich web-based resource listing issues to consider when creating a fund to support APCs.

HYBRIDS

Indeed, one issue to be addressed with centrally managed APCs is whether the fund should favor fully OA journals over the hybrid variety. Many journals are primarily subscription/license based but offer the author an option of paying an APC to make their individual articles OA despite most of the papers remaining behind a paywall. Because these APCs represent a second source of income (in addition to subscription/

license) for the same journal, many hybrid publishers have pledged to provide a commensurate reduction in subscription fees, either to an institution whose authors have paid APCs, or generally across the board. Some in the scholarly communication community have made efforts to verify whether hybrid publishers have reduced subscription price corresponding to OA fees paid by authors. So far, the results are not impressive, but it may be due to administrative burden as much as anything else. It may be easier for an individual organization to verify a reduction in journal subscriptions if they can account for OA fees paid by their authors, but nonetheless, it may turn out to be too burdensome for most libraries to take on. In any case, educating authors who publish via the "hybrid" option to this potential for double dipping by publishers should be a part of the conversation between science librarians and authors.

A related service to managing APCs centrally or establishing a fund for APCs is the creation and management of memberships with OA publishers such as PLoS or BioMed Central. Generally, these large OA publishers offer organizational memberships which results in a lower APC for authors who are affiliated with the organization. Presumably, a calculation of how many articles have typically been published (and paid for) by the organization weighed against the publisher's membership fee and corresponding reduction in APCs would demonstrate whether this kind of service is worthwhile. This data would of course be more readily available where there was a faculty database of publications (as described above) but again, the administrative overhead of managing a program like this must be included in any calculation of financial sustainability. While the library might be the logical place to do this (because of their facility with bibliographic data), it would require some dedication of time and staff.

Providing funding for OA APCs is not as simple as it may sound. First, eligibility requirements have to be set and undoubtedly there will be some who feel they are too restrictive. Reimbursement mechanics are typically complicated. To expect the library to pay the publisher may be unrealistic for a number of reasons. Sometimes fees are collected upon manuscript submission and if the paper is ultimately rejected, there has to be some way to return or account for the funds.

Finally, many librarians feel that OA fund creation is largely created out of existing library budgets and that providing this money to researchers means that there is less money for acquisition of library materials. Still, assuming a continued reduction of in-library visits, growth in the self-help model of science libraries, and the central collection of research publication metadata, this shift of resources seems like it would be worth exploring as a library service.

SUMMARY: INFORMATION AND AWARENESS

In recent years, a proposal for revolutionizing the scientific publishing business has gotten more than passing notice. First articulated by librarians at the Max Planck Institute, it holds that the aggregate total of all journal subscriptions paid worldwide adds up enough to pay the APCs for all individual papers to be published under an OA model and freely available. The total expenditures by research institutions (whether journal subscriptions or APCs) would remain nearly constant, but the benefit would be that the articles would be openly accessible, the theory goes. There is some debate about the specifics and viability of such a proposal, but in this case, the role for the science librarian is to at the very least inform his or her user community that such a debate exists and start them thinking more about a system that they have likely taken for granted for a long time.

As mentioned earlier, the lack of information about the price of journals that scientists depend on the library to provide is likely a major contributor to rapid price increases. Informing readers of the particularly egregious price increases is in some sense doing a "service" to the scientist because s/he can then make better decisions on where to publish their work or serve as reviewer or editor and to advise their graduate students on the same topics. It also may spur them to think about journal title, publisher, or impact factor as a proxy for quality and whether a journal in a given discipline with subscription twice as high as another in the discipline is truly twice as valuable, all other things being equal (e.g., number of papers, number of issues, etc.)

When journal cancellations are inevitable, the science librarian can defer to hard data to support their choices. Cost-per-download data for a given institutional subscriber is available from most journal vendors and/or from other services. Collecting the number of times a particular journal is cited by an institution's researchers is also a valuable piece of information when deciding on journal cancellations. This information can be obtained via one of the citation indexes or in a custom report from a commercial provider. When doing this investigation in-house (using Web of Science or Scopus or some other tool), it is possible that variations in the institution name will surface in the index being used. This can be a good time (given resources) to try to standardize the institution name in the commercial database. This may be helpful in other service areas such as institutional research metrics. Presenting this data to scientists is in a sense speaking their language in which it represents a systematic and careful analysis of activity and not a conjectural or anecdotal basis for decision-making.

And while the widespread adoption of organizational standard identifiers may make this job unnecessary one day, there will still be plenty for the librarian to do in support of scholarly communication. Perhaps, the greatest service science librarians can provide for their scholars is an interest in and knowledge of the changes in the scholarly publishing world. It sends the message that she is aware of what they do besides read the articles and books she has purchased, and it shows a professional dedication to furthering the mission of the organization and of science.

REFERENCES

Coalition for Networked Information, 2017. Rethinking Institutional Repository Strategies: Report of a CNI Executive Roundtable.

Dempsey, L., Malpas, C., Lavoie, B., 2014. Collection directions: the evolution of library collections and collecting. portal: Lib. Acad. 14 (3), 393−423.

Hirtle, P., 2006. Author addenda. D-Lib Mag. 12 (11), . Available from: <http://www.dlib.org/dlib/november06/hirtle/11hirtle.html> (accessed 19.09.16.).

Jones, P., 2016. Getting the measure. Research Information (December2015/January2016). Available from: <https://www.researchinformation.info/feature/getting-measure>.

Jubb, M., 2016. Libraries and the support of university research. In Quality and the Academic Library: Reviewing, Assessing and Enhancing Service Provision. <https://doi.org/10.1016/B978-0-12-802105-7.00014-2>.

Kennison, R., Shreeves, S.L., Harnad, S., 2013. Point & counterpoint: the purpose of institutional repositories—green OA or beyond? J. Librariansh. Scholarly Commun. 1 (4), eP1105. Available from: <http://jlsc-pub.org/articles/10.7710/2162-3309.1105> (accessed 19.09.16.).

Kronman, U., Lundén, A., 2013. Can open access create a sound scholarly publishing market? ScieCom Info 9 (2), . Available from: <http://journals.lub.lu.se/index.php/sciecominfo/article/view/7298> (accessed 19.09.16.).

Laakso, M., Welling, P., Bukvova, H., Nyman, L., Björk, B.-C., Hedlund, T., 2011. The development of open access journal publishing from 1993 to 2009. PLoS ONE 6 (6), e20961. <https://doi.org/10.1371/journal.pone.0020961>.

Mullen, L., 2010. Open Access and Its Practical Impact on the Work of Academic Librarians: Collection Development, Public Services, and the Library and Information Science Literature. Chandos Pub, Oxford.

Niu, X., et al., 2010. National study of information seeking behavior of academic researchers in the United States. J. Am. Soc. Inf. Sci. Technol. 61 (February), 869−890. <http://doi.wiley.com/10.1002/asi.21307>.

Salo, D., 2008. Innkeeper at the roach motel. Lib. Trends 57 (2), 98–123. <https://doi.org/10.1353/lib.0.0031>.

Scholarly Publishing and Academic Resources Coalition (SPARC), 2007. Campus Open Access Funds—SPARC. Available from: <http://sparcopen.org/our-work/oa-funds/>.

Sinn, R.N., Woodson, S.M., Cyzyk, M., 2017. The Johns Hopkins Libraries open access promotion fund: an open and shut case study. Coll. Res. Lib. News 78 (1), 32–35. Available from: <http://crln.acrl.org/content/78/1/32.full>.

Sterman, L.B., Clark, J.A., 2017. Citations as data: harvesting the scholarly record of your university to Enrich Institutional Knowledge and Support Research. Coll. Res. Lib. 78 (7), 952–963. <https://doi.org/10.5860/crl.78.7.952>.

CHAPTER 4

Publishing Services

> Library-based publishing programs are pragmatic responses to evident needs, not services in search of clients, ... Library publishing is not a movement so much as a development
>
> *Hahn (2008)*

When the Internet began to offer easy-to-use tools for users to generate content, new opportunities emerged that made the network more than just a one-way communication medium. Web 2.0 brought blogs and media sharing sites, and it wasn't long before it became clear that individuals with few resources could nonetheless create content that could be widely distributed and that had an audience. As with most Internet phenomena, the application of user-generated content was adopted a bit later in academia than in the consumer world, but when it took off, it was purpose-driven. Almost concurrently, the increasing unaffordability of scientific journals became more widely known. Some of those involved in scientific research saw an opportunity to solve a problem of the accessibility of peer-reviewed scholarly output by using emerging, available, and relatively easy-to-use web 2.0 tools.

ORIGINS OF MODERN LIBRARY PUBLISHING

The serials crisis of the 1990s led to the open-access (OA) movement which in turn resulted in developments such as library-based publishing as an alternative to high-priced journals. During this period, several professional associations and societies formed consortia or other efforts as they sought alternatives to budget-breaking journal subscriptions. At one Association of Research Libraries (ARL) meeting, members agreed to pool resources to fund a more affordable and sustainable publishing model after years of exorbitant journal price increases, and in 1998, they created the Scholarly Publishing and Academic Resources Coalition. Among other things, this resulted in the creation of BioOne, a staple of affordable digital resources familiar to most life science librarians today. Soon, several other projects such as Project Muse (Johns Hopkins and Cornell) and

HighWire Press (Stanford) exploited available digital tools and platforms in an effort to ameliorate rapid inflation among periodicals. A later effort of particular interest in the STEM community includes Project Euclid (Cornell and Duke Universities) which provides support to small mathematics and statistics society publications in order to keep them affordable. And as recently as 2017, the formation of the not-for-profit, Scientific Society Publisher Alliance shows that there is still a desire to provide high quality and affordable research.

The development of publishing services in libraries was further supported by small publishers who were dissatisfied with trends in the publishing world. Societies and associations have been contracting out their journal operations to commercial publishers for years, but smaller societies have often found the cost too high and had to remain print-only or find other partners. Publishing operations with a small portfolio of titles found that the economies of scale had not yet been reached for conversion to online production. In other cases, journals in certain subdisciplines may have had such a narrow appeal that commercial publishers did not foresee an adequate return in taking on these titles.

As is often the case with new library services, it is the larger institutions that have led the way in library publishing efforts. Reports from ARL and ITHAKA (Hahn, 2008; Housewright and Schonfeld, 2008) showed a professional interest in publishing by academic libraries and that large university libraries began the trend by undertaking a variety of publishing activities. The ARL report revealed that 65% of the member libraries had or were planning on some form of library publishing operation in the near future with nearly 1000 journals being produced by library-led publishing operations in 2014 (Busher et al., 2014).

But information technology costs tend to fall quickly at the same time usability improves, making what was once restricted to the wealthy and/or sophisticated soon accessible to a much wider community. Lower cost and lower technological barriers have allowed smaller research libraries a greater opportunity to offer publishing services to their institutional community. Some library publishing efforts have provided a solution for small and niche journals to move online, and the results have been impressive, among them a greater readership and recognition of the journal (Busher and Kamotsky, 2015).

The creation of the Library Publishing Coalition (LPC) in 2012 also demonstrates a growing and sustained interest among librarians in taking on publishing services. At its inception, more than 50 libraries joined the

LPC, and it has grown to include over 70 members as of 2018. Their *Library Publishing Toolkit* is essential background reading for any librarian interested in offering publishing services. It includes case studies and service ideas for both public and academic libraries and is available online or in print. The *Toolkit* looks at contemporary library publishing and showcases opportunities for libraries to create and provide access to content.

REPOSITORIES

Another of the trends that has fostered the development of library publishing is the creation of institutional repositories—a phenomenon which is also traceable to the serials crisis and the OA movement. The proliferation of repositories has taught scientific organizations (and perhaps librarians themselves) that research outputs can be collected, filtered, and disseminated locally and flexibly. The affordability and ease of use of repository software means that costs to distribute and manage digital research materials has fallen sharply, again drawing the interest of researchers and the institutions which generate this content. Where library publication programs have been established, the services often (and most successfully) were embedded with other services including repositories, copyright advisory, digitization programs, and digital preservation (Hahn, 2008; Furlough, 2010).

LIBRARY—PRESS PARTNERSHIPS

In addition to supporting small-society publishing, some science librarians have found common ground with their institutional press. Much has been written about the financial plight of university presses due to their heavy reliance on subsidies and the narrow readership of academic monographs. At the same time, there have been more and more university presses administratively reorganized to report to the library. As university presses' dependence on monograph sales revenue leads some to doubt their sustainability; library-publishing operations can provide some support for institutional presses via one of the several models. Some believe that online publishing of print editions results in greater sales of print copies.

Like many other publishers, university presses are moving their content online, albeit a bit more slowly since they tend to concentrate on monographs and there has not been an established business model for electronic books outside of the commercial, for-profit publishers. Where university presses do publish journals, partner libraries have some experience and facility to help.

Library—press partnerships may involve digitization of current titles or expansion of content to accompany print or digital titles. The inclusion of multimedia or additional images (where space in the print publication does not permit) is another area where science librarians can offer service to the press and the community of potential readership.

Many partnerships between libraries and institutional presses have had success in the digitization of the press' legacy print collections (Brown et al., 2007). While monographs tend to be used less among scientists, there are still some classic works in the sciences that can be converted to digital form. These are often out-of-print or titles with very low-sales volume. In many cases, the libraries with established scanning operations and experience converting print to digital have provided this service, while the press provided rights and permissions management. While it might seem that this cuts into the potential sales revenue of the press (where print titles are still available), these efforts do not seem to affect sales of these titles (Crow, 2009). In some cases, the material is restricted to the institution's user community as in the case of the University of California's eScholarship Editions.

LEGACY CONTENT REPUBLISHING

Among the simplest library-publishing projects that can be undertaken is the digitization of institutionally or society-published materials that had been previously issued in print. This backfile digitization requires not just assembling the content, compiling the metadata, and coordination the scanning. On an administrative level, it entails documenting rights and terms from the original publisher and securing funding not only for the immediate production process but for the sustainable hosting of the content.

Backfile republishing has been done successfully on both a large and small scale. Among the more notable examples are the University of California's UC Press eBooks Collection, 1982—2004, the University of Pittsburgh Digital Editions, and the consortial, Biodiversity Heritage Library (BHL).

Digitization of backfile material can be particularly applicable where the science librarian's institution is home to or closely associated with a scientific society—perhaps one founded by former scientists of the librarian's institution. In addition, a disbanded or now-defunct society which published a journal or report series which may not have been widely distributed in the print era but are nonetheless in demand today might be a strong candidate for digitization.

As mentioned earlier, one example of a large backfile-publishing program is the BHL. This content is the result of a consortium of natural history and other scientific libraries which have identified public domain works for digitization and, in addition, negotiated republication rights for some still-in-copyright books and journals. Many of those works which are still protected by copyrights were published by societies which are too small to scan and host their legacy journals and reports themselves but are happy to see it incorporated with a larger digital library like the BHL. In addition, this material is mirrored in other services such as the Digital Public Library of America (DPLA). Because BHL members have established digitization operations, these materials which had previously seen limited use can now be made more widely available via the BHL. With consortial digitization or the integration of locally scanned publications into larger efforts such as the DPLA, there is a network effect where the value of the content is significantly enhanced simply because it is included in a larger body of literature that has an established user base.

While publishing a contemporary journal often requires an online editorial and manuscript management system, digitally republishing backfiles can be done with only a server and an open-source software platform for viewing, searching, and perhaps browsing the content. One of the easiest solutions for hosting this type of material is to use an existing institutional repository, if available. The commonly used repository platforms such as DSPace, Digital Commons, or ePrints offer an out-of-the-box solution for presenting bibliographic information and corresponding digital text and incorporating it all cleanly into the wider online scholarly community. Many of these platforms include search engine optimization, a standard method to expose the data for harvest by other service providers, and some statistics on readership or downloads, including time period or geographic area. Digital Commons in particular is a tool that is widely used for library-publishing operations.

METADATA

Adequate article-level metadata is of course ideal for scanning and hosting journals. Scanning whole volumes is better than nothing, but where there are separately authored chapters within the volume, the optimal solution would be to scan each bibliographic unit into a separate file with its own metadata. Obviously the same would be true for journal volumes containing distinct issues and/or articles. Scanning at the article level may create additional work for the digitization process but makes the content much more discoverable and useful than simply digitizing each volume in a single file. This may not always be possible but should be considered when beginning a conversion from print to digital as it ultimately aids in discovery and usability of the content.

To increase site visits, discoverability, and the overall profile of the material, it would be ideal to export or offer the metadata to standard abstracting and indexing (A&I) services and of course to scholarly search engines. If a printed edition of scanned materials has already been indexed by these services, the science librarian could work with the A&I vendor to add URLs [or digital object identifiers (DOIs) if the library creates them] to the index record so that users can be made aware of the online availability of what was previously available only in print. This will likely also require some forethought regarding metadata consistency and completeness.

In addition to standard bibliographic metadata, scientific publications often belong to disciplines that have their own vocabularies, structured terms, or unique identifiers. Scientists and their informatics counterparts use concepts to refer to or classify publications that may not be included in traditional descriptive metadata. It is common to find online resources built and maintained by scientists which use these otherwise unfamiliar metadata schema, and where applicable, it might be worthwhile for the science librarian to incorporate them into publishing efforts. Examples include biodiversity information (such as that collected by the Global Biodiversity Information Facility), crystallographic compound, or genetic sequence information. These terms or identifiers may not be intelligible to an undergraduate taking an entry-level science course but are meaningful and very useful to scientist, especially when it augments the corresponding published literature.

Marking the library-published material with these terms and identifiers is more tedious than a simple print-to-digital conversion but the effort may pay off as it tends to ensure findability, usage, and integration with a wider scholarly community. This can have knock-on effects such as raising the profile of the home institution, the science library undertaking the publishing effort, and perhaps the cultivation of financial support from scientific societies and organizations which find this text enhancement worthwhile. Librarians who investigate the incorporation of special terms and taxonomies into digitized content should also consider employing some kind of semantic markup of the text if there are agreed-upon or recognized standards for the scientific discipline. Marking the text in a machine-readable way will ultimately make it more valuable and easily integrated into emerging online systems in research computing. Again, this takes time and effort, but a proof-of-concept project may cultivate financial support for the idea.

METADATA SEARCH, RETRIEVAL, AND DISPLAY

Like any academic content posted on the web, it is desirable to ensure that it is findable where scientists generally look. And these days that means Google Scholar (GS). Marking up content with metadata to ensure that it is included in GS search results is critical to the success of the library-publishing operation. Most science librarians have seen scientists treat GS as a first and only stop for search. The exact markup required for indexing in this universally consulted source has changed over the years, and it may not be clearly articulated, but many repository and publishing platforms include tools to ensure proper markup.

In addition to this, it is wise to expose the publication metadata in other formats. The Open Archives Initiative Protocol for Metadata Harvesting (OAI-PMH) standard has been around for a while and is still used by many services. Commercial library discovery services routinely ask for content to be exposed in this manner, and science librarians who have become involved in publishing should remember to contact their service provider to see if their digital collections can be included not only in the home library discovery search but also integrated into the provider's larger body of work for other organizations to search and find. Again, many repository and publishing platforms ensure OAI-PMH compliance, but library staff should ensure that it is activated and periodically verify that it is working and that harvest is happening.

We have been hearing for some time about the semantic web where markup of content is much richer and integrated, and the use of linked open data, RDF, and other formats are designed to foster those goals. Where possible, library publishers should investigate whether the markup of content using one of these metadata applications is possible, and if not too time-consuming or costly, implement one of them. Schema.org has examples of markup that is fairly simple to understand and test.

It may be worth experimenting with website analytics before and after applying one or more of the metadata schema to validate the operation. But one thing is clear, publishing operations are largely unsuccessful if the content cannot be discovered as widely as possible and that requires complete and standard metadata to ensure discovery across multiple platforms.

In addition to publication design and layout, library staff should address which metadata elements could (or must) appear on the item landing page and/or on the PDF, assuming one is stored or generated from the publication site. These elements might include a running article title, journal title, DOI, and/or URL, and perhaps a recommended citation. In addition, one of the article pages may include ISSN or a license statement [e.g., Creative Commons (CC) terms].

RIGHTS AND PERMISSIONS

Before digitization and metadata preparation takes place, science librarians may need to secure rights and permissions from the publisher or current rights holder (if they can be identified). In the United States, public domain material covers everything published prior to 1923, so if there is any legacy scientific content available to the science librarian via institutional archives or affiliations, this may make a good first step into library publishing. In other cases, outside assistance may be necessary. Some librarians may have access to legal counsel, but where formal review and transfer of rights are not possible (especially in the case of out-of-print, society published material), a memorandum of understanding (MOU) or some other letter of mutual agreement between the rights holder and the library can at least serve as a starting point if any disputes arise in the future. As with all legal matters, it is best to document as much and as early as possible.

Many library-publishing efforts are undertaken in the spirit of OA with no cost assumed for the reader or user. This generally means that operating costs are borne by the parent organization, a funding body, grant, partner organization, or some other benefactor. However, when certain content—particularly books—are converted from print to digital, it is not uncommon to find that third parties have downloaded and post the content for sale on external websites. Although trying to sell something that is freely available elsewhere may seem fruitless, it is nonetheless done by less-than-honorable web entrepreneurs whose costs are undoubtedly small enough to make even very low sales volume worth the effort. Librarians and rights holders might want to address this in any MOU including excusing the library from any culpability or responsibility besides the duty to notify interested parties when this comes to their attention.

It may be beneficial to specify a license for library-published material even if it leaves very few restrictions. CC has several standard licenses that library-publishing managers should be familiar with. Each specifies permissions for reusing the data. This may not stop the most unscrupulous from doing what they will but as with all things legal, it is a good idea (and represents little effort) to put one of these licenses in place and to display it on the publication website and on either the display page for each item or the page footer, etc.

Always be sure to verify whether you have rights to reproduce all contents contained within publications, especially where images or other material for which rights are not retained by the institutional publisher or partner society may be included.

REFERENCE MATERIAL

In addition to the inclusion of discipline-specific vocabularies and concepts in publishing articles, conversion of certain reference material into a searchable database is another way that science librarians can augment material currently available only in print. Lists of specimens, laboratory notes, or other catalog-like entries from well-known projects from the past can be marked up and converted to a reference tool to make the material much more useful than when originally created. Marking entries as linked data and/or including links and references to published works can be particularly valuable to scientists. The information may have already been compiled into a reference book or it may consist of only raw, tabular data. But converting it to digital form allows search, sort, and filter on this information as well as a much wider distribution than the print edition had.

The conversion of this tabular data to an online database may involve tasks beyond the responsibility of the librarian such as data entry or rekeying into parsed fields. But the science librarian can act as project manager, gauging interest, securing funding, finding a vendor to convert the text, establishing some form of quality review, etc. to ensure that the electronic publication of this reference material is done properly. It may be beneficial to have the vendor mark this material up as linked data so that it is more easily integrated with other web content. This is beneficial to the project, but care should be taken in exploring common vocabularies and ontologies so that the exposure of this information is leveraged to the greatest extent possible.

ALTERNATIVE FORMATS

At the opposite end of backfile republishing is the hosting and management of preprints. In recent years, this seems to be an increasingly popular option for scientists. Where the physics preprint server, ArXiv, was the leader and practically the sole player in this space, the last few years have seen the creation of a biology preprints server (bioRxiv), the emergence of ChemRxiv, and the effort to integrate many others that appear to be taking hold (Callaway, 2017).

Like many scholarly communication services in libraries, preprint servers are more of a service for authors than for readers. Because these papers are not yet reviewed, many scientists will not cite them formally. However, preprint servers do provide a method of establishing scientific priority as the initial upload date can be used to determine the exact date on which a scientist and his/her team made their claim(s). And while these preprints may not be a fodder for formal citation, they can nonetheless inform others as to progress the research in their field and help form directions, hypotheses, etc. (Vale and Hyman, 2016).

Preprints servers tend to be discipline-specific and not institutionally based. This confirms the lesson from institutional repositories which shows that many scholars feel a greater affinity and responsibility to their scientific discipline than to their parent organization. However, an awareness of preprints and the benefits and availability of these services are areas that librarians involved in publishing can and should develop. Assistance in identifying preprint servers and even describing and uploading content is something that librarians can provide as a service. It should be noted that the granddaddy of preprints servers, ArXiv, is currently hosted at Cornell University Library.

In addition to efforts at OA, libraries have become involved in publishing in part due to their willingness to embrace experimental or new forms of scholarly communication (Hahn, 2008; Crow, 2009). Because these may be formats which are outside of traditional peer-reviewed articles, acceptance of these formats by scientists and research evaluation and review bodies might mean their development is slow. However, librarians should be prepared for a possible transition of research products as traditional documents to multifaceted digital objects which take full advantage of the platforms on which they are housed, discovered, and read (Tracy, 2015).

A variety of non-journal content can be published by libraries including datasets, locally created content such as papers from an organization-hosted conference or other research outputs that do not fit the journal article model. In the sciences, printed copies of doctoral dissertations may be kept by the library but rarely distributed beyond friends and associates of the graduate and sponsor. Digital publishing of this material is an opportunity to support institutional research but may require some rights and permissions legwork. In the case of theses and dissertation republishing, be sure to respect the institution's privacy policies, for example, by redacting or removing the author's personal information such as address, phone number, etc. There should also be a review for third-party content (e.g., images) contained in dissertations where permissions would prevent republishing the content.

DATASETS

It is probably the publication of datasets that will receive the most emphasis in coming years. Because data collection is the most labor intensive part of scientific research, this core activity may soon be recognized and rewarded in proportion to the effort taken. We see the emergence of data journals as evidence of this. In addition, the automated generation of articles based on scientific data is likely to become more widespread in the near future in many respects, not the least of which is the use of natural language processing as is increasingly used in news reporting. In the commercial world, the use of robots to write human-readable text is used for internal communications and commercial publications (Hutchinson, 2018). The progression of the application of technology to academia will likely see its growth after it becomes firmly established elsewhere.

Datasets are fast becoming mainstream citable research outputs. This is shown by the emergence of the data journal where there is little or no analysis and in which the articles tend to be shorter, emphasizing methods and leaving it up to the reader to interpret the data. The increasing requirement for data-management planning means that this material will become more and more intelligible (if only to machines) but reusable and therefore publishable. The topic of dataset publishing not only deserves its own book but also deserves mention in any discussion of library publishing efforts.

REGISTRATION SERVICES

For any digital content published at the science library's institution, it is desirable to create DOIs. Most science librarians are aware of the benefit of using DOIs in bibliographic data management as they help to integrate scholarly content into the broader online publications world. What many librarians may not know is the ease with which they can provide this service whether to their institutional press or to any other publishing operation that takes place in their organization.

Normally, identifiers for journal publications are registered with CrossRef (http://crossref.org) which charges a nominal annual membership fee a cost for each DOI created. Currently, this fee varies depending on whether the item is contemporary or a DOI is being registered for a legacy publication that has perhaps been digitized only recently.

Another publishing registration service with which librarians should be familiar is the creation of ISSNs. For journals published by the librarian's organization, there should be a corresponding ISSN. Because the popular DOI registration authority for publishers, CrossRef currently requires that metadata for journal articles includes a journal ISSN, the registration of a journal is the first step in offering DOI services. In the United States, registration of a journal to obtain an ISSN is free via the Library of Congress, but the procedure may not be the one with which the institutional publication office staff are familiar. Librarians, because of their familiarity with such systems and associated information, are an obvious choice to provide this service.

HOSTING SERVICES

Another fairly straightforward publishing support service that science libraries can (and increasingly do) provide is coordinating the hosting of digital materials. Libraries with existing repositories can leverage their platform depending on user requirements to serve digital publications whether generated by the library or a partner organization. But where the library-run institutional repository does not meet user needs, repository management experience often provides enough knowledge and expertise to explore additional platforms which are more specifically created for publishing.

Among the more popular publisher platforms that libraries can manage are the Public Knowledge Project's suite of products such as Open Journal Systems (OJS) or Bepress' Digital Commons. With OJS, it may be possible to coordinate a local installation with institutional IT services, but if local support is not available, server and software can be provided by Public Knowledge Project (PKP) for a relatively low annual fee. Digital Commons provides a hosted repository and digital publications platform which is used by over 500 research organizations. In either case, external hosting allows the library to limit service to metadata management, digital content management, identifier (such as DOI or ISSN) creation, and the coordination of integrating the content with internal and external services, leaving the technology support to another organization.

DIGITAL PRESERVATION

Libraries offer postproduction services to institutional publishers, among them the management and preservation of digital editions. The use of LOCKSS (https://www.lockss.org), for example, ensures that a digital version of an institutionally published journal will remain available even if disaster (natural or organizational) happens. Science librarians can work with an institutional or society publisher and LOCKSS to ensure that their digital content is archived. This is as important as integrating metadata with other collections and services, since it not only preserves the journal for the future but also because LOCKSS is a distributed system, it may also cultivate wider recognition of the publication.

PLANNING, ADMINISTRATION, AND MANAGEMENT

Like all service development, library publishing operations should consider financial sustainability. But that is not always the path taken. It is common for new library services to start at a grassroots level with a librarian identifying a need (and a consequent legacy activity which can be reduced to allow time to shift focus). And while there is some appeal to allowing microservices to grow to assess their viability, strategic planning for the eventual success of the enterprise is a worthwhile effort. It is important to keep these activities in mind when doing strategic planning or budgeting exercises, even if it is understood that some will inevitably fail. But failure is all but assured if the emergence of new services is not supported for by management.

With some exceptions, it is common for science librarians who become involved in publishing operations to be employed at large universities and/or work with a university press. However, even where that is true, funding for publishing operations in the library is not assured. The 2008 ARL survey of publishing activities, for example, revealed that few had adequately budgeted for sustainability of the program (Hahn, 2008). The financial and institutional commitment to library publishing is often higher than what many small organizations can sustain, except where publishing operations are well defined and discrete and where the content being published appeals to a niche user community. Small starter projects are often undertaken as one-time efforts but can soon turn into other opportunities and become continuous activities. Some efforts, such as Project Euclid, depend on a subscription model and revenue from external clients (Furlough, 2010), but this seems to be the exception. Where publishing activity requires subscriber or other external monetary support, a partnership with an existing press or other business unit is desirable. But whenever possible (during proof-of-concept and prior-to-service development), the business model or economic support should be considered by the program manager and his/her director.

FUNDING

Many library publishing operations depend on sponsorship either built into the library budget or from a partner or parent organization. Most desirable of course is the assurance from all parties that this funding is assured for the foreseeable future and not grant-dependent or otherwise paid for with fixed-term funds. Where short-term funding is unavoidable, some effort at continual fundraising (via internal or external resources) is inevitable. Many scientific organizations and associations have competitive intramural grant and award programs, and receiving funding from one of these sources may be easiest at first and provide experience for library staff who lack experience in seeking grant funding.

Some library publishing operations, particularly where a partnership with an existing academic or university press exists, can pursue revenue source from sales. The collection of payments represents an administrative burden and often conflicts with a library and research organization mission, but where the partner press has an established cost recovery component, it may be easy for the library staff to build this into their budget. Still, managing subscriptions, credit card payments, or IP-based access to digital editions may be something that neither library nor PESS staff are equipped to manage. There may be service providers to handle this, but of course there would be fees involved and some assurance that these fees would be offset is necessary.

SKILLS

Nobody can provide services which require skills for which they have received no training. However, many publishing activities require knowledge that librarians have acquired natively over the years, especially those regarding metadata and digital content management. In addition, web markup or at least a rudimentary knowledge of CSS or HTML is helpful in creating readable content, and many organizations have these skills internally if not within the library.

Finally, why should libraries become involved in publishing operations? This new kind of service offers a chance for libraries to develop partnerships with research departments at the organization. Increasingly academic libraries are turning toward the collection, description and accessibility of research produced at their home institution and making it available to the rest of the world. This is in contrast with the traditional model of collecting externally generated materials and making it available to users at the home institution (Dempsey et al., 2014). Publishing operations also increases the library's visibility at a time when visitorship is down and one might argue that the library is becoming increasingly "invisible."

REFERENCES

Brown, L., Griffiths, R., Rascoff, M., 2007. University Publishing In A Digital Age, New York. ITHAKA 69 p. <https://doi.org/10.18665/sr.22345>.

Busher, C., Kamotsky, I., Taylor, A., 2014. Library-Led Publishing with Bepress Digital Commons: Data and Benchmarks Report. Bepress, Berkely, CA.

Busher, C., Kamotsky, I., 2015. Stories and statistics from library-led publishing. Learn. Publ. 28 (1), 64−68.

Callaway, E., 2017. Heavyweight funders back central site for life-sciences preprints. Nature 542 (7641), 283−284. <https://doi.org/10.1038/nature.2017.21466>.

Crow, R., 2009. Campus-Based Publishing Partnerships: A Guide to Critical Issues. SPARC, Washington. Available from: <http://sparc.arl.org/resources/papers-guides/campus-partnerships>.

Dempsey, L., Malpas, C., Lavoie, B., 2014. Collection directions: the evolution of library collections and collecting. portal: Lib. Acad. 14 (3), 393−423.

Furlough, M.J., 2010. The publisher in the library. In: Walter, S., Williams, K. (Eds.), The Expert Library: Staffing, Sustaining, and Advancing The Academic Library in The 21st Century. Association of College and Research Libraries, Chicago, pp. 1−30.

Hahn, K.L., 2008. Research Library Publishing Services New Options for University Publishing. Library, 1−41. Available from: <http://www.arl.org/bm ~ doc/research-library-publishing-services.pdf>.

Housewright, R., Schonfeld, R., 2008. US Faculty Survey 2006: Studies of Key Stakeholders in the Digital Transformation in Higher Education. <https://doi.org/10.18665/sr.22367>.

Hutchinson, A., 2018. Robotics Takes on Scientific Publishing. Digital Science. Available from: <https://www.digital-science.com/blog/guest/robotics-takes-scientific-publishing/>.

Tracy, D.G., 2015. The users of library publishing services: readers and access beyond open. J. Electr. Publ. 18 (3), <https://doi.org/https://doi.org/10.3998/3336451.0018.303>.

Vale, R.D., Hyman, A.A., 2016. Priority of discovery in the life sciences. eLife 5, e16931. <https://doi.org/10.7554/eLife.16931>.

CHAPTER 5

Research-Information Management

Because of an increasing attention to return on research investment, both scientific organizations and those that sponsor their research have recently expanded efforts to account for outputs under their oversight or sponsorship (Moed, 2011; Kramer, 2010). Efforts at translational science and an increasing emphasis on public engagement by scientific research organizations have also prompted efforts to document research activity, communicate research to nonscientific audiences, and pursue exposure of scientists and their work outside of traditional press releases or social media. This effort to raise public awareness of the scientific research being done at the organization may ultimately yield benefits in terms of fostering a network of scientists outside the organization, recruiting postdocs, and other students or early-career scientists, potentially enhancing the possibilities for external funding.

The increase in cross-discipline collaboration and the exposure of scientific accomplishment to external audiences have given research information systems (RISs) a good deal of notice. Among other ways, this is apparent from the emergence of commercial and open-source products launched in recent years to meet this need including several traditional library vendors. These vendors typically have had an access to a very large body of scientific literature (Jacobs, 2016), and it seems like a natural progression of product development for them to move into this area. Existing relationships with librarians has meant that science librarians have frequently been facilitators of the implementation of these services at research organizations.

[*A note about terms: this type of service is still developing and consequently we see several terms used to describe systems in place. Similar efforts are variously called faculty reporting systems, current research information system (CRIS), research profiling or research networking systems, but in any case they describe the same kind of service: the collection of information describing the research done by scholars at a particular organization. For simplicity, I will use research information system (RIS) system to describe the technologies that are in use across research organizations today*]

Science Libraries in the Self-Service Age
DOI: https://doi.org/10.1016/B978-0-08-102033-3.00005-2

HISTORY

As scientific publishing and related systems became digital, standardized, and interoperable, the collection of research outputs has become easier. Since the early 2000s, several efforts have been launched to systematically and uniformly capture organizational research information. EuroCRIS was created in 2002 to foster knowledge exchange and interoperability among current RIS (CRIS) in part by establishing the Common European Research Information Format (CERIF). Many European countries conduct nationwide research evaluation exercises, and the CERIF standard was a natural outcome.

Later, as part of the 2009 American Recovery and Reinvestment Act (ARRA), the US government began an effort to quantify the economic benefits of federally funded research. The result was STAR Metrics, an effort to develop measurements for the economic impact of scientific research by collecting data on outputs and outcomes. Another result from the ARRA was the creation of eagle-i, a system to collect and share information about biomedical research, facilities, and collections. These and other efforts have cultivated an awareness of both the need for and increasing ease of creating and using RIS.

Perhaps, the origins of library involvement in RIS stem from their work with institutional repositories (IRs) in the first decade of this century (Givens et al., 2017). IRs were an attempt to collect the formal research output of an organization to both archive and share this activity with a wider scholarly community. However, the early experience with IRs showed that many scientists may have a greater affinity for their professional discipline than for their parent organization as shown in their willingness to embrace discipline-specific repositories over their home IR (Salo, 2008). Some repository managers and their software platforms responded to this lack of enthusiasm by trying to implement profile pages for authors in the repository which offered a more personal representation of a scholar's works.

Today, a RIS can retrieve information based on research publications, grants, courses, datasets, laboratories, geographic locations, funding agencies, and other rich material that would perhaps require an afternoon of tedious search, download, and assembly of data were it not collected in one place. There are several software options for RIS including commercial, open-source, and home-grown, mirroring somewhat the evolution of IR platform development.

USE CASES

RISs can serve multiple purposes, making it an appealing service to develop since a wider potential audience can mean greater recognition for the library. However, these multiple user communities may bring a variety of sometimes conflicting needs. When planning or implementing this kind of system, science librarians should bear in mind the distinct user communities (scientists, policy and administration, communications and fundraising among others) and tailor their communication to each. And while the model of entering data once and reusing multiple times is appealing, each of these user groups may have slightly different needs that place restrictions of demands on the service which may not be palatable to everyone. Some groups may want to record not just research outputs but mentions in the media (or in social media). Others may want to list awards and recognition, while others concentrate on grants, specifically money brought into the organization. The inclusion of journal impact factor may be important to some but not all stakeholders. These competing interests must be made aware of one another and the need to negotiate in order to develop the best product for the organization.

SCIENTIST PROFILES

Among the most common and recognizable application of RISs is its use in profiling researchers, their outputs, and expertise; in redisplaying research information on other organizational websites; and in research evaluation and metrics. Such a system can also serve to document the use of labs, research stations, or other shared facilities in order to evaluate return on investment.

Expertise locator and expert profiling systems help promote research outside the organization, but they may also be used to help internal audiences identify and locate experts on a particular subject area. Research organizations such as universities commonly contain silos of information which are not widely shared, and this makes it difficult to locate people within the institution who have a particular knowledge or expertise. A RIS, by aggregating some of this information, provides a single place to identify and locate research interests at the organization.

Faculty or researcher profiling systems can appeal to a varied audience at a research organization beyond administration and research policy groups. Communication and related offices at scientific organizations are always interested in an easy method to discover research activity at the institution to quickly answer queries, both internal and external. Fundraising and development offices use these systems in a variety of ways, for example, to create a speakers' bureau where they can identify scientists who may be willing to talk about their research to potential donors and/or at fundraising events. Donors who wish to support research in highly specific subject or geographic areas benefit from the RIS and presumably the scientist and his/her program may find previously unknown sources of support.

For the scientist, research profiling systems can serve as a network to establish connections with others in their field and be discovered by potential collaborators or mentors/mentees. RIS which are public-facing not only allow organizational publicity but also can allow graduate students, postdocs, fellows, and other scientists to identify individuals with whom there may be a partnership developed for research collaboration.

Some RIS can include information not only about people but also about laboratories and research facilities. Information on the output associated with these can be valuable to research administration as it shows return on the resources invested in the facility.

EVALUATION AND METRICS

Another core function of these emerging systems is for research reporting, evaluation assessment, and metrics. Here, the audience is primarily the upper administration of the parent organization. European universities are accustomed to standard research evaluation and reporting exercises, and RIS serve this purpose. Even outside of European countries where research evaluation is conducted on a national level, universities and research organizations are finding that RIS provide a useful service but where a need was never clearly articulated.

ENTER ONCE, REUSE OFTEN

The single point of collection but multiple reuse of this data is another key idea behind RIS. Everyone agrees that entering the same information twice—even by different people—is inefficient, and for this reason, systems such as a RIS that reuse the same data in multiple ways tend to receive support. This central repository of metadata can be reused on websites so that the data is leveraged for the additional purpose of populating information on individual or departmental web pages. In addition, where possible, the implementation of a one-click curriculum vitae (CV) generation tool is another strong incentive for scientists to become active in at least the review if not the entry of data into their RIS profile. Some RIS platforms offer customized CVs and templates, and it may be worthwhile developing an output template for this data to create a biosketch suitable for NIH or NSF grant applications. The SciENcv bioSketch structure is one that some RIS can handle since it is required of grantees from those agencies.

For redisplay of this content on other organizational websites, the RIS in a sense may serve in part as a kind of content-management system if the data can be pushed from the RIS to the website in an automated (and near real-time) basis. This method of easily adding to and editing content on their websites might mean that scientists become more invested in institutional RIS since they may be more directly affected and can see immediate results of edits they make. Reuse of the data is one of the ways to directly and immediately demonstrate value of RIS to researchers who may otherwise view the system as an unnecessary administrative burden.

DATA COLLECTION

Because information that is included in RIS often comes from disparate sources within a research organization, it is likely that some of these data suppliers will be considered the source-of-record, and the RIS is only a subset or copy of the original data. One example would be the data maintained by an institution's office of sponsored research (or similar office where grants and awards are tracked). A research-information management team often establishes a regular export or feed of information from this and other sources to keep the RIS current. But for various reasons, it is unlikely that the RIS will be the authorized version of this data. For that reason, a system should be established to update the data when records are changed in the source. This requires some coordination of effort to ensure that duplication does not occur but that the data are as closely synchronized as possible.

In addition, the RIS (especially in the case of grants) will probably not include all information from the source database, and the system should only be used for general inquiry, referring to the source-of-record database for more precision when needed. One advantage of most RIS available today is accessibility: they are much more searchable and user-friendly than typical institutional databases which are kept for historical and administrative purposes.

The ingestion of data to a RIS system depends largely on the sources of the data at the research organization. Publication data is fortunately becoming more standardized with public APIs to collect and format for import and has therefore never been easier to collect (Bryant, 2017). But local content such as grants, courses taught, awards, etc. may have to be entered by hand or reformatted regularly for import. RIS system administrators should evaluate the trade-offs for importing data or for entering by hand. In either case, data collection often requires some data manipulation and certainly some notification to data suppliers that the content will be reused. It also can frequently bring attention to what might be poor quality source data that may or may not be welcome news. Some institutions have gone scientist-by-scientist and entered (by hand) information from their CV including educational information. The bottom line is as follows: for the RIS to be useful, it will need to be kept up to date, and this should be accounted for in the planning.

As mentioned earlier, most early IRs were largely untouched by the scholars they were intended to help. And it is becoming common to see the same thing with RIS. However, features such as biosketch or other CV generation, and the reuse of data on individual web pages should provide some incentive for scientists to at least review if not update the content in the RIS.

SENSITIVE DATA

One thing to keep in mind with a public-facing RIS is that there may be some scientific work being conducted at the organization where the details are better kept private. Examples might be biomedical facilities and/or personnel where animal subjects are used in laboratory or other experiments. Likewise, the identity or location of sites where ancient artifacts or endangered, exotic or otherwise valuable plants and animals are found should perhaps be scrubbed from any site that the public can access.

It is common for RIS implementations to find anomalies, inconsistencies, and other problems with source data created by the home organization. In fact, publication data may be the most reliable thanks to standard metadata and the use of identifiers. Human resources, grants data, and other sources, because they are not originally created with reuse in mind, may frequently need review, enhancement, or other manipulation before being imported into the RIS. This can sometimes require manual editing, but even a partial automation of this reformatting is best whenever possible. Bear in mind that most imports will have to be repeated over time (at least in part) and that the steps to manipulate this data should be recorded so as to be done uniformly. It may be helpful to explain the data sources on the RIS "About" page or include a short disclaimer statement in the page footer noting that much of the data comes from elsewhere and that it is only as reliable as the source data, etc.

COMMON VOCABULARIES

As with all metadata solutions in libraries, it is important to adopt standards to make systems as interoperable as possible. Even where the RIS is intended for internal use only, it is not impossible that one day the data will be shared with the larger scientific research community, and the use of standard vocabularies and hierarchies to describe an institution's research activities is highly desirable. Two efforts (among many) stand out in the area of standards for RIS: the CERIF and the Consortia Advancing Standards in Research Administration Information and are worth investigating. Some systems have adopted the VIVO Integrated Semantic Framework ontology which uses concepts and relationships applicable in most common university and research settings.

RDF AND INTEROPERABILITY

Aside from these specialized taxonomies, RIS also store and display bibliographic data as well as geographic and other standard data. Geographic data in particular is useful to apply to research outputs as it allows the easy identification of individuals doing work in a particular region of the country or the world. Several RIS platforms have geo-mapping plugins or other features, making it useful to collect this kind of metadata.

Some RIS platforms leverage the collection of data by presenting it as linked data (Nonthakarn and Wuwongse, 2015) which has the potential to make information about one research organization easily integrated with others who likewise use linked data formats. In fact, the use of this format to enable cross-institution connections was expressed in an early tagline for the VIVO software: "Enabling National Networking of Scientists."

Science librarians may not be expected to understand this data structure and how to work with it, but if their organization tests or implements any of the RIS platforms which use linked data, they may begin to see how this format can be leveraged to create a network of scientists across the globe in which many scientists would be eager participants. One example is a program sponsored by the DDRI of the Research Data Alliance called ResearchGraph. This is a set of tools "designed to connect datasets across multiple platforms by co-authorship or other collaboration models such as joint funding and grants" (ResearchGraph, 2017).

CURRENT RIS SOLUTIONS

There are a variety of ways to collect and disseminate information about scientific research activity taking place at a particular organization. As with most classes of software, some are easier to implement than others. Some may be developed in-house or commercially provided and hosted. Some may be easily integrated with other systems and others freestanding and largely isolated. A detailed document listing required features will make the selection of the RIS platform much easier and more effective.

FREE SYSTEMS

Although not providing most of the required features of a standard RIS, there are freely available services which have gained some popularity among scientists although their service and user community are different than those of the commercial services listed below. Google Scholar, for example, invites researchers to create a personal account where their publications are added seamlessly from the Google Scholar index. This also includes some statistical data such as number of times one's papers have cited and the author's H-index. Google Scholar collects and attributes publications to profiles, but the connections can be erroneous. Scientists sometimes view their profile in Google Scholar and wonder why a certain paper is listed as one being coauthored by them. This is easily remedied, but one needs to continually view his/her profile to catch these somewhat rare errors. It should be noted that many of the commercial products also use some algorithm to match publications with authors, but most require some form of acknowledgment or "claim" by the author (or his/her designee) before it will be added to the scientist's profile.

ResearchGate (RG) is a social network site for scholars to upload the full text of their papers (including an automated method) and to share them openly or on a case-by-case basis. Users can also upload datasets, connect with others, find jobs, and view statistics on who has been reading their work. At a very basic level, it serves as not an institutional but rather an individual repository of reprints. They can be made public or released on demand to those who request them. Individuals who use RG have their publications indexed in Google Scholar making this information easily findable. Users can add keywords or concepts to their profiles, their education, and research positions. Organizations such as departments and labs can be created, and users affiliate themselves with them. RG is quite popular with over 3 million users, and because it is indexed by Google, the content is extremely accessible. The appeal of the site is to the individual scientist and not the institution. Some information is aggregated, but none is available for download.

Worth noting is that Google Scholar and RG are free and lack any transparent business model, and it should therefore be recognized that either could be discontinued at any time. It may be worth the librarian's time to remind scientists of the standard caveats about free Internet services where the "product" may in fact be the data which is collected about users. Also, Google Scholar and RG do not provide the expert locator service for a given organization that other RIS do and do not provide a method to reuse this data on web pages. Mentioning them here is mainly to respond to scientists at an organization which is implementing a RIS and who may counter that they don't need such a service because they already have a Google Scholar or RG account and wonder why they need another one.

COMMERCIAL SERVICES

Several traditional library vendors have begun to offer products that can be categorized as CRIS and/or research-information management. This appears to be a logical progression in service development from vendors which have historically sold abstracting, indexing, and citation analysis tools to libraries. As self-service tools like Google Scholar and PubMed emerged, these traditional abstracting and indexing providers appear to have begun to recognize a slightly different audience at research organizations, perhaps due to a migration of users to these free indexes.

The increasing emphasis on research metrics, evaluation, and return on investment has led scientific organizations to employ some form of bibliometrics, and companies such as Clarivate, ProQuest, and Elsevier have met this need. Their access to a large body of article literature may have allowed these firms to develop systems to analyze and manipulate this publication data and to create research evaluation and metrics tools which generally serve not scientists in search of peer-reviewed papers, but those in science policy and administration. This enables a high-level review of the research conducted by a particular scientist, laboratory or institution. Clarivate was the early leader in this space, with tools such as InCites and other products designed to measure research outputs, collaborations, and offer comparisons between institutions and countries. But others followed with similar products.

Soon these companies released RIS platforms as enterprise-wide solutions, some of which are broken into modules and may be licensed separately. These might include award management, reporting, importing, multi-format CV generation, etc. The products, Pure (Elsevier), Converis (Clarivate), and Elements (Symplectic), each meet very similar needs of research institutions but with some variations. The emergence of these kinds of services from traditional and familiar library vendors means that librarians should not ignore the opportunity that RIS provide for becoming more involved and engaged with scientists and administrators at their organization. It can also be taken as further evidence that library services are rapidly evolving in response to the commodification of scientific journal literature.

OPEN-SOURCE SOLUTIONS

In addition to some commercial and freely available products, there are open-source options available to research institutions that have a need to collect and manage research outputs. The two most prominent are VIVO and Profiles RNS (Research Networking Software). VIVO was originally developed at Cornell University and today in use at over 150 research institutions. It allows organizations to collect research outputs for individual scholars or organizations and present them in a customized way. Many science and other research libraries are active in the implementation of VIVO and the population of data such as staff publications, grants, courses taught, lectures, prizes, and other notable biographical information of the kind one might find on a typical scientist's CV.

Profiles RNS was developed originally as part of an NIH grant but is used most heavily by biomedical organizations. Profiles RNS (originally known as Harvard Profiles reflecting the affiliation of the original developers) shares a vocabulary with VIVO which is important in ensuring interoperability. The VIVO community hosts a conference each year in the United States which is often attended by Profiles RNS user institutions.

The popular DSpace repository platform also presents an open-source option for research information collection and management. In 2009, a collaboration between DSpace users from Hong Kong University and 4Science-created DSpace-CRIS, an extension to the popular repository software that extends description and collection beyond publications to other research entities (e.g., organizations, events, people, etc.)

PARTNER WITH OTHER ORGANIZATIONAL UNITS

The success of a RIS with multiple audiences and multiple sources of data frequently depends on the participation of groups beyond the library. As with most technology solutions (especially open-source tools) implementing a RIS requires some assistance from those with pure information-technology skills. The institutional IT or academic-computing department should be involved early in any discussion and planning for this kind of effort. Librarians are most helpful in identifying data sources to be ingested into the system, filtering and reformatting the data where needed, establishing or selecting metadata standards, and cultivating support and interest not only among scientists but other audiences on campus. It is also important for all participants in the planning and implementation of an open-source software solution to remember that although the software itself is free and without any paid license to use it, there are often significant costs involved, and despite having what may be a large and helpful user community, support for these platforms is done largely on a volunteer basis.

There are often firms which support open-source RIS platforms, and these services may be considered in the implementation of an open-source RIS. Commercially available platforms normally provide support and upgrades; however, there will almost always be a need for some IT support from the home institution, if only to automate the query, ingest, and update of data from institutional data sources. Webmasters will also want to know how and in what format the RIS exposes or makes data available for reuse, and the standardization of this data reuse is important for widespread adoption across web platforms if more than one is in use at a scientific organization.

Another candidate partner for RIS implementation is the office of sponsored research (or office which tracks extramural funding). Their database will be one of the primary sources for most RIS, and it is best to at least inform them that some of the data will be reused. Creating a routine to harvest, reformat, and ingest data from their system regularly is ideal, but initial efforts may require some manual cleanup. It is possible that the public display of some of this data may be objectionable to certain parties and policies should be discussed and clarified early.

And of course the organizational administration (who will ultimately pay for this service) and individuals who will be listed in the system should be involved both in planning and rollout.

USE OF IDENTIFIERS

The use of persistent, unique identifiers can facilitate implementation of RIS by scientific organizations. These can apply to individuals as with ORCID iD or DOIs for publications or locally managed identifiers for organizations and other entities. When leveraging a RIS system to become a networking tool, it is becoming essential that these commonly used identifiers are incorporated in an organization's metadata.

RIS implementations have been characterized by librarians as "cataloging people" and that may be one of the reasons for the strong appeal as a new service option (Warren and Rauh, 2017). For this reason, many of the commercial and open-source products include the ORCID iD as a standard metadata element to describe and exchange information about scholars with publishers, databases, and the ORCID system itself. Publications, grants, and other research outputs may be collected in many different places, and the use of ORCID iDs can facilitate the movement of this data to the RIS, thereby relieving all from the tedium of reentering or manually capturing this information. In addition, while actual compliance and use may differ, most scientists declare support for both researcher identity systems such as ORCID as a means of disambiguation and crediting scholarship accurately and for researcher-networking systems (Tran and Lyon, 2017). If possible, it may be best to implement these persistent identifiers farther upstream, for example, in the sponsored programs database (for individuals, funding bodies, or grants themselves) or the OHR system of record to uniquely identify scientists. However, that may not be feasible given existing (legacy) system constraints. Undoubtedly, an internal organizational identifier (such as a university or employee ID number) will be used and connected via local database somehow to the scientist's ORCID iD.

But along with the unambiguous identification and description of individuals, RIS often include information about organizations, both internal and external. The inclusion of information about external organizations can be useful in preparing for or reporting on collaboration and funding, and otherwise working with external partners. A standard of unique identifiers for organizations is emerging in the same spirit as ORCID iDs for individuals. GRID, ISNI, and other parties uniquely identify organizations which might otherwise be listed with various forms of their name, abbreviations, and, most vexingly, without hierarchical context. Librarians can often work with the issuing organization for these identifiers to remove duplication or ambiguity and perhaps establish some hierarchy among the departments, laboratories, and their parent organization.

Internal organization identification can also be important when assessing the use and value of certain research facilities. Where publications and other research outputs can be associated with laboratories, research stations, and other satellite facilities, this may provide easy dashboard-like reporting to administration that want a quick sketch of productivity in these organizations. The use of standard organizational identifiers makes this easier. Recently, ORCID has begun working with several government and research organizations and publishers on a Publications and User Facilities Task Force to help in assessing the scientific impact from investments in research facilities used by outside parties. These facilities (laboratories, research stations, equipment, etc.) often are the result of public (taxpayer) investment. But reporting on research outputs associated with the use of such infrastructure and equipment is difficult. The task force is trying to determine what data would help agencies and facilities document this and how ORCID might enable the collection of such data. This might become another identifier which the science librarian could facilitate for his/her home institution which would appeal to research and other administration.

IMPLEMENTATION AND PARTICIPATION

Many RIS engage in proactive collection of data about research outputs, primarily publications and grants. It is no secret that many (but certainly not all) scientists consider the manual entry of publications into an IR to be tedious at best and annoying for most. The use of ORCID iDs by individual authors may facilitate automated data harvest which, while welcome by everyone, is nonetheless not perfect.

Because many bibliographic databases serve as sources for the data, there is inevitably duplication and false hits, all of which have to be individually selected, accepted (claimed), or rejected. It is here that the standardization found in the biomedical publishing infrastructure is most effective. Because Medline (and subsequently, PubMed) have been in development for so long and because they have had strong support from many organizations and individuals, the automated harvest and matching of publication data is most extensive and most accurate in biomedicine and related disciplines.

Piloting with certain groups (if possible) can be a valuable investment of time as it can point out flawed processes, user needs, and scalability that may not have been apparent during the planning or implementation discussions (Givens et al., 2017). Discovering these requirements or needs for improvement early will contribute to the potential success of the program rather than launching institution-wide.

SUMMARY

The collection and reporting on research activity is increasingly important in organizations doing scientific investigation. RISs have emerged as a viable solution, and implementation often involves the science librarian for reasons of skills and existing relationships at the organization. However, the involvement of other units, particularly data contributors, end users, and of course the scientists themselves, is critical for the success of these systems. In particular, the scientist must receive some tangible benefit fairly early in the implementation to ensure their participation. Commercial and open-source solutions exist, many of them offered by traditional library vendors due to their access to a large body of bibliographic data. The use of identifiers and standards adopted by publishers, research organizations, and associated players makes this data more available and usable than ever before. Science librarians who see a reduction in traditional library service used by their community should consider participation (if not leadership) in RISs; however, expectations should be well managed and realistic goals created in order to ensure eventual success.

REFERENCES

Bryant, R., 2017. Making sense of the confusing world of research information management. Research Information Systems: The Connections Enabling Collaboration. NISO. <http://www.niso.org/news/events/2017/2017_virtconf/aug16_virtconf/>.

Givens, M., Mackllin, L.A., Mangiafico, P., 2017. Faculty profile systems: new services and roles for libraries. portal: Lib. Acad. 17 (2), 235–255.

Jacobs, N., 2016. Research information management. Digital Information Strategies. pp. 57–69. <https://doi.org/10.1016/B978-0-08-100251-3.00004-4>.

Kramer, D., 2010. Initiative aims to quantify the paybacks from basic research. Phys. Today 63 (8), 20–22. <https://doi.org/10.1063/1.3480067>.

Moed, H., 2011. Research assessment 101: an introduction. Res. Trends (23), 3–4.

Nonthakarn, C., Wuwongse, V., 2015. An application profile for research collaboration and information management. Program 49 (3), 242–265. Available from: https://doi.org/10.1108/PROG-02-2014-0007.

ResearchGraph, 2017. Retrieved from: <http://researchgraph.org/>.

Salo, D., 2008. Innkeeper at the Roach Motel. Lib. Trends 57 (2), 98–123. Available from: https://doi.org/10.1353/lib.0.0031.

Tran, C.Y., Lyon, J.A., 2017. Faculty use of author identifiers and researcher networking tools. Coll. Res. Lib. 78 (2), 171–182.

Warren, S., Rauh, A., 2017. Creating a culture of research reputation through research information management systems. Research Information Systems: The Connections Enabling Collaboration. NISO.

CHAPTER 6

Data-Management Services: Advocacy, Communication, and Policy

Like research, data management is a team sport

Heather Coates (2014)

Despite the self-service nature of science libraries today, there remain tasks that scientists do as part of their research that could be facilitated by librarian assistance. If we consider the scientists' complete research workflow, they spend only a small part of their time retrieving literature to support their work. And while they may enjoy catching up on current publications in their field, there are other more pressing things they are required to do (Flaxbart, 2001). That includes writing both papers and grant proposals, managing their research materials (print and digital), running a laboratory or field work, hiring and supervising graduate students, and doing other administrative tasks. More and more librarians recognize the need to understand all of their scientists' research activities (Shaffer, 2013), and as they do, one thing becomes clear: publication output is a primary concern of scientists and leaves little or no time for data curation and the creation of associated metadata (Jahnke et al., 2012). But forward-thinking librarians are beginning to develop services to meet this gap, especially with regard to advice, planning, and/or managing digital research data.

Increasingly, scientists are required to create data-management plans (DMPs) in support of their grant application (California Digital Library, 2010). Several US and UK government agencies which sponsor scientific research now require data-management planning as a component of the grant application process, and many private endowments have followed suit including the Gordon and Betty Moore and the Alfred P. Sloan Foundations. This shows that those who sponsor scholarly research are beginning to require primary investigators to think about and document their intentions for the data for which the sponsor has paid. It is believed

Science Libraries in the Self-Service Age
DOI: https://doi.org/10.1016/B978-0-08-102033-3.00006-4

that making data reusable by others may support future research where the same data can be used perhaps in answering different and unrelated research questions.

The emphasis on metrics, return on investment and objective evaluation of scientific research is forcing the scientific community to look at new ways of measuring impact. Research impact has traditionally been measured by publication and citation counts, but shared datasets represent a relatively new form of recognized scholarly research output. With the current changes to the scholarly publishing world and the influence of open access, sharing, and collaboration, the data a scientist collects may ultimately be more valuable in terms of research recognition than the papers he or she authors (Coates, 2014; Pool, 2016).

In fact, it is possible that the dataset will become a publication-type standard along with articles, chapters, and books (Ware and Mabe, 2015, p. 139). The increase in what are called data journals demonstrates the increasing importance of data sharing in this exercise. These journals are often descriptions of scientific datasets whose primary purpose is to describe data, rather than to report a research investigation in contrast with the traditional peer-reviewed scientific journal (Chavan and Penev, 2011). The Ecological Society of America, American Chemical Society, and Springer-Nature are among several respected organizations which publish a regular data journal. Some scientists are beginning to believe that having one's data cited could one day have greater professional value than having one's paper cited (Fane et al., 2016).

The science librarian, because of his or her close contact with scientists, is probably the best resource for first-hand review of current practices and deficiencies in research data-management (RDM) services. The creation of other scholarly communication services such as repository and metadata collection should provide a reason for the scientists to remain engaged with the librarian and perhaps provide a stable relationship from which to launch more advanced services such as RDM. Otherwise, scientists may continue their drift into the self-service sphere, and library mediation becomes no longer necessary.

NEEDS ASSESSMENT

Establishing an existing need for any new service seems like something that is self-evident at the concept stage, but a needs assessment is a worthwhile exercise. Identifying specific needs (and not just creating an RDM program because other research libraries are doing it) can quickly inform and focus the development of services, potentially saving library staff time, and effort. Identifying key scientific staff who are creating and want to share research datasets is the first stop in a needs assessment. The organization's office of sponsored research or similar office which coordinates extramural awards can identify recent grantees. From a list of recently awarded grants, the librarian can then discuss informally the work of the scientist including potential data collection, capture, etc. Because many scientists have not been trained or prepared to address their data needs in any formal way, the expression of interest by another person (in this case, the librarian) can often result in eventual cooperation in service development—even if rudimentary at first.

It is worth noting that funding information is increasingly available via bibliographic tools such as CrossRef and commercially produced indexes to scientific literature. This is too late for data-management planning since the grant is likely completed, but the identification of previously awarded grants (when not captured at the point of award) can be a good conversation starter and indicate interest and willingness of library staff to become involved in the research life cycle outside of traditional literature acquisition, storage, and retrieval.

A list of funding bodies sponsoring research at the institution can be compared to a list of funding agencies which require DMPs. It may be worthwhile to suggest that any extramural grants database managed by the office of research include a list of funding agencies which require DMPs (supplied and maintained by the science librarian), and this can be used to more easily generate reports on principle investigators (PIs) who face this requirement. The identification of RDM needs will be much easier in any case if the library establishes and builds a relationship with the office which monitors grants and awards.

With this list of scientists who recently faced the requirement to create a DMP, science librarians can create a survey to establish gaps where needs are not being met. The survey can be created with known organizational and cultural practices in mind and/or sample questions which are available from colleagues at other libraries which have begun the process already. Many research libraries have posted results of their surveys on their websites, and this may be informative in creating an RDM needs assessment where sample questions are not readily available.

Another path toward needs assessment is to find what datasets have been archived and shared from a given institution. Searching an

organization name in DataCite, Dryad, or other well-known data repositories, while it may yield false hits, will nonetheless show a sample of
datasets which have been created by scientists at a particular place. This
information can not only provide an opening to dialog between librarian
and scientist but may also provide examples of material to be documented
in an institutional research output or metrics database.

PLANNING, BUDGET, AND INSTITUTIONAL SUPPORT

When beginning any new service, it is always a good idea to document
the needs, current practices, and expected or desired results so that success
can be clearly demonstrated. This may seem a burdensome administrative
task, but where RDM is sorely lacking, it may quickly become obvious
that there is a gap between what is and what should be done.
Documenting this along with desired outcomes is an essential project-
management procedure and, among other things, allows for the evaluation of the success of the effort.

In addition, it is tempting to start small and hope that as its popularity
grows, financial support for a new service will follow. Because formal
RDM is fairly new to librarians and most (but not all) scientists, initiation
of services can be done slowly and still provide noticeable benefits to the
research organization. Microservices, while seemingly minor, can meet
just enough requirements to cultivate an appreciation and momentum for
service development. But while a small, well-defined service may be
readily implemented in the short term (and a commonly used strategy to
build data-management services), an awareness of eventual resource need
should be articulated as early as possible, if only to serve as a placeholder.
Preliminary steering or planning committee notes or meeting minutes
can provide this information; it does not have to be formal.

Research data is a valuable asset to an institution and it should be recognized that data-management costs money. On the other hand, it should
also be pointed out that the cost to an organization which fails to adequately manage data could be greater than is generally recognized (Erway
and Rinehart, 2016).

Building data-management costs into grant proposal budgets seems at
first to make a lot of sense. Funding agencies after all are the ones who
most often create the requirement to archive and share the research data
they are paying for, so they should bear at least some the expense of
ensuring that these requirements are met. But while costs for preparing

the data during the research process can be included in a grant budget, ongoing costs cannot. Funds for RDM can be included in the indirect costs portion of a budget, but other units often depend on this money, and it may be difficult for an institution to change its calculation and distribution of indirect costs to redistribute funds to those units (such as the library) providing RDM services (Erway and Rinehart, 2016).

Offering RDM services through the library can be done with varying degrees of intervention. There are "concierge" or referral services which merely point a scientist to existing resources where s/he can find help. Or a librarian could become deeply involved in documenting, moving, and managing files as part of the research team. In either case, it is best to do some preliminary assessment of needs and of resources required to meet the various levels of needs. Libraries which have existing repositories of texts and articles authored by scientists at their institution should be aware that managing a data repository is often much more costly than a reprint repository (Beagrie et al., 2008).

When libraries offer RDM services, it is often in collaboration with other units such as IT, the office of sponsored research, and the science units themselves. These offices can at the very least provide background on existing resources and help with proactively identifying grant PIs who may be required to create (and follow through with) a DMP. Where collaborations are established, it may be helpful for some organizations to define the extent of responsibilities so that roles cannot become distorted which is sometimes a tendency with new service types (Coates, 2014).

ADVICE AND POLICY

Science librarians who want to begin offering RDM services have a variety of opportunities before them. Many scientists and their teams are unaware of data-management policies and mandates or are unwilling to undertake the effort due to a number of factors, resource scarcity being primary among them (Ware and Mabe, 2015 p. 141; Ferguson 2014). In fact, the White House Office of Science and Technology Policy memorandum on public access to federally funded research materials specifies that federal scientific agencies should identify "resources within the existing agency budget to implement" their plan to share data. However, it continues that agency plans should "allow the inclusion of appropriate costs for data management and access in proposals for Federal funding for scientific research" (Holdren, 2013).

It is important to remember in planning RDM services that there may be some scientific work being conducted at the organization where certain details should be withheld from public view. Open science is of course the goal, but, for example, where details on animal subjects being used in laboratory or other experiments or the identity or location of sites where ancient artifacts or endangered, exotic, or otherwise valuable plants and animals are found is included in datasets, this information should be kept private and released only after vetting by the data stewards/owners.

Beside the need to comply with data sharing and archiving mandates of funding and other institutions, scientists may benefit from knowing about additional tools which make planning and sharing of datasets easier and more affordable. Increasingly, scientists learn of data-sharing policies of journals and/or funders who support their research. But it can be frustrating when instructions for deposit and resources to comply are not included. Librarians can help by identifying repositories which meet the mandate criteria and any repository-specific policies, fees, deposit mechanics, and other details that scientists often feel they lack time for. These are basic advisory services which the library community can provide in support of this goal.

AWARENESS SERVICES

An awareness by science librarians about who in their organization is collecting scientific data, on what subject, and in what general format is the key to evaluating the possibilities for RDM services. A detailed picture of scientists' research has been cumbersome in the past as librarians have been limited to an anecdotal recollection of the books and articles requested by a researcher. Due to the multiple channels that scientists use to retrieve their literature, a review of reading material may provide only an incomplete picture of a scientist's research interest. But an awareness of recently awarded grants is an often overlooked source of information on current research being conducted at an organization and can be a good basis on which to explore the possibility of RDM services.

Occasionally, scientists may be skeptical of librarian involvement in RDM, and it is important for science librarians to do their homework before approaching the researcher, PI, or data collector. Knowledge of policies, metadata, repositories, and what others (within or outside the home institution) have done or are doing is essential for the science librarian to know before contacting scientists regarding potential RDM services. This awareness demonstrates to the scientist a familiarity with the issues and allows the librarian to quickly get to a discussion of these with the right people. It serves not only the scientist but also the librarian, as it completes a picture of the scientist's research and doing so early enough for more services to be developed and provided.

DATA-MANAGEMENT PLANS

Funding bodies which sponsor scientific research see the potential reuse by future scholars of data generated as one form of return on their investment. Understandably, some scientists consider this new requirement to be burdensome and not something with which they have experience or an established routine. Librarians understand the components for managing digital material through their experience with repositories, their use, and a growing understanding of unique identifiers and robust metadata all of which can make creating a DMP easier for scientists.

By providing publicly available boilerplate DMP generation tools as well as the language to use and an outline of points to address, science librarians can go a long way in serving scientists who are unfamiliar with the requirements and too busy to think about it. Implementing DMPTool[1] is not only a way to both encourage and assist in data management but also to brand the library and its services. The DMPTool is provided by the California Digital Library and provides researchers a guided means of creating a DMP. Because the plans created by the Tool can be made public (or hidden), users can sometimes review other DMPs and/or share their own.

In addition, research organizations can become DMPTool partner institutions and create custom templates for their researchers to use. Science librarians may want to consider creating a custom DMPTool template for their organization based on input from scientists and administration. Member institutions can incorporate custom language such as the description of their institutional repository, its specifications and compliance with standards, as well as suggested answers to data–management questions for users. Compliance with DMP creation can be further facilitated by coordinating institutional sign into the system using the credentials for the user's home network access.

[1] https://dmptool.org/.

Creating a DMP as a required element of a funding application is one thing, but actually following through on describing, sharing, and archiving scientific data represents work that scientists have not done traditionally and for which there is often no immediate remuneration (although a well-planned grant application may include resources necessary to address data management). It might be expected that once scientists create a DMP, actual follow-through on the plan (much like depositing their publication in an institutional repository) is just a distraction from the next research project which has often already begun before closure of the current project.

Some research organizations have stated that they will be responsible for their scientists' compliance with data-sharing mandates from federal funding agencies, and this may be an area where librarians may be able to help, for example, by documenting DMPs and associated grants. Where research data is archived in a repository outside the scientist's home institution, specific criteria, or even specific repositories could be documented with regard to whether they meet certain minimum specifications. This kind of list would also support compliance efforts that research organizations undertake.

RETENTION AND APPRAISAL

One thing is clear to anyone becoming involved in managing research data: there is a lot of it and imagining potential future use is highly speculative. Librarians feel that we can estimate the utility of books or journals which we add to our libraries, but because datasets are so narrow in focus, it may be hard to imagine a person who might find any particular file or files useful. This is where archival practices come into consideration. Most archives have schedules to retain or dispose of records—it is unrealistic to keep everything, after all.

Research data is no different. There is no reason to believe that all data should be retained forever. In fact, DMPs can and should include a statement of retention period both to emphasize to the funding agency that maintaining this material in perpetuity is not sustainable and to demonstrate that the PI has thought about all of the issues. Retention and disposition of material are often associated with archivists and not librarians, but the management of research data may be an illustration of how the jobs of both are subject to change.

Several guides have been written by established data curation and archival bodies on appraisal and retention of research data including the Digital Curation Center[2] (DCC), the Natural Environment Research Council, and the University of Bristol among others. The comprehensive DCC appraisal guide has a page listing the steps to consider in appraising research data for retention or disposition. Scientists, while they may balk at devoting time and resources to managing and documenting their research data, nonetheless often feel that it should be maintained forever. Science librarians should prepare for this where needed by documenting costs of open-ended storage and management of the content and describing the scale across the home institution to illustrate the need to be realistic about these needs. Potential future use should be weighed against costs, the latter of which may not be easily understood by scientists.

Among the issues to be considered when evaluating a research dataset for retention is whether the data is reproducible. Obviously, something like climate data which is collected and is specific to a certain time period cannot be reproduced. Also, data that has come from tissue samples (plant or animal) may not be easily reproduced due to the difficulty of obtaining tissue samples again either from the same species or from organisms that otherwise have identical characteristics.

Certainly, funder policies on retention should be considered in the data life span. Among other things, best practices as stated by the US Geological Survey are to determine if there are any legal or policy requirements regarding the data. Of course policies by funding agencies or institutions may be as unrealistic about open-ended costs of preserving research data as many scientists. It should also be noted that selection of a specific repository may have to include factors such as temporal agreements and arrangements.

TRAINING AND SKILLS DEVELOPMENT

It will be necessary to develop new skills and possibly new career paths among library and information science studies to fully embrace RDM services (NSF-ARL, 2006) To that end, there are several data-management certification programs at schools of library and information science including at the University of North Carolina, Syracuse University, and an online program from Simmons College. In addition,

[2] http://www.dcc.ac.uk.

workshops have emerged where librarians frequently attend alongside data scientists and laboratory and other project managers (Data Carpentry, 2016; University of Edinburgh, 2016).

Finally, no preparation for RDM services could be called complete without visiting and reviewing the DCC website. This site was established in 2004 in response to a JISC document calling for a center for "solving challenges in digital curation that could not be solved by any single institution or discipline." Although it was established for the UK Higher Education community, most of its resources are applicable internationally.

REFERENCES

Beagrie, N., Chruszcz, J., Lavoie, B., 2008. Keeping Research Data Safe: A Cost Model and Guidance for UK Universities. London: Higher Education Funding Council for England. Available at: www.webarchive.org.uk/wayback/archive/20140615221657/http://www.jisc.ac.uk/media/documents/publications/keepingresearchdatasafe0408.pdf.

California Digital Library, 2010. DMP Requirements. Retrieved from: <https://dmptool.org/guidance>.

Chavan, V., Penev, L., 2011. The data paper: a mechanism to incentivize data publishing in biodiversity science. BMC Bioinf. Available from: http://doi.org/10.1186/1471-2105-12-S15-S2.

Coates, H., 2014. Building data services from the ground up: strategies and resources. J. eScience Librarianship 3 (1), 52–59. Available from: https://doi.org/10.7191/jeslib.2014.1063.

"Data Carpentry Workshops.", 2016. <http://www.datacarpentry.org/workshops/> (accessed December 13).

Erway, R., Rinehart, A., 2016. If You Build It, Will They Fund?: Making Research Data Management Sustainable. Retrieved from: <http://www.oclc.org/content/dam/research/publications/2016/oclcresearch-making-research-data-management-sustainable-2016.pdf>.

Fane, B., Treadway, J., Gallagher, A., Penny, D., Hahnel, M., 2016. Open season for OpenData: a survey of researchers. The State of Open Data Report. Digital Science, pp. 12–19. Retrieved from: <https://figshare.com/articles/The_State_of_Open_Data_Report/4036398>.

Ferguson, L., 2014. How and why researchers share data (and why they don't). Retrieved from: https://hub.wiley.com/community/exchanges/discover/blog/2014/11/03/.

Flaxbart, D., 2001. Conversations with chemists. Sci. Technol. Lib. 21 (3–4), 5–26. Available from: https://doi.org/10.1300/J122v21n03_02.

Holdren, J.P., 2013. Increasing Access to the Results of Federally Funded Scientific Research. Washington, DC. Retrieved from: <http://www.whitehouse.gov/sites/defaul/files/microsites/ostp/ostp_public_access_memo_2013.pdf>.

Jahnke, L., Asher, A.D., Keralis, S.D.C., 2012. The Problem of Data: Data Management and Curation Practices Among University Researchers. Council on Library and Information Resources.

National Science Foundation, & Association of Research Libraries, 2006. To Stand the Test of Time: Long-Term Stewardship of Digital Data Sets in Science and Engineering | Association of Research Libraries® | ARL®. Retrieved from: <http://

www.arl.org/publications-resources/1075-to-stand-the-test-of-time-long-term-stew-ardship-of-digital-data-sets-in-science-and-engineering#.WFBa7dVpGmw>.

Pool, R. 2016. Dare to share? | Research Information. Research Information, (December). Retrieved from: https://www.researchinformation.info/feature/dare-share.

Shaffer, C., 2013. The role of the library in the research enterprise. J. eScience Librarianship 2 (1), e1043. Available from: https://doi.org/10.7191/jeslib.2012.1043.

University of Edinburgh, 2016. Research Data MANTRA. Retrieved from: <http://datalib.edina.ac.uk/mantra/> (accessed 13.12.16).

Ware, M., Mabe, M., 2015. The STM Report: An Overview of Scientific and Scholarly Journals Publishing. Oxford. Retrieved from: <http://www.worldcat.org/oclc/932410520>.

FURTHER READING

Read, K.B., Surkis, A., Larson, C., McCrillis, A., Graff, A., Nicholson, J., et al., 2015. Starting the data conversation: informing data services at an academic health sciences library. J. Med. Libr. Assoc. 103 (3), 131–135. Available from: https://doi.org/10.3163/1536-5050.103.3.005.

CHAPTER 7

Data-Management Services: Practical Implementation

It is really only a matter of time before having a highly-cited dataset is as important in some fields as a paper in Nature, Science, or Cell. . .[1]

Daniel Hook

HANDS-ON WORK

In addition to policy, compliance, and referral services regarding research data management (RDM), science librarians are also becoming involved in the day-to-day activities around data collection, formatting, and description. For deposited data to be useful and usable by others, it must be described accurately, both for discoverability and so that once found, data can be understood and used by other scientists. However, the reuse of scientific data is not yet well documented (Pasquetto et al., 2017), and the primary motivation for sharing data still seems to be well-intentioned mandates by funding organizations to leverage their investment to further scientific advancement.

Because the recognition of the importance of RDM has only reached a wide audience in recent years, it is not only librarians who are novices in this domain. Scientists themselves, their assistants, and students, while they are familiar with their own data and practices, nonetheless often lack a clear picture of what well-managed datasets look like.

Among the simplest (and often the initial) practical RDM services provided by libraries are those that follow from existing support for scholarly communications. For example, it is increasingly common for a scientist, upon acceptance of his or her manuscript, to be asked by the publisher to make the supporting data for the paper available to readers in a public-facing repository. Scholarly communication services providers in libraries are familiar enough with publishing practices to meet this need. Meeting this publication requirement normally involves identifying a

[1] Quoted in: Pool (2016).

Science Libraries in the Self-Service Age
DOI: https://doi.org/10.1016/B978-0-08-102033-3.00007-6

repository (whether at the home institution or outside) and ensuring that the data is adequately described and identified so that it can be discovered and reused. Some journals archive the data on their own website or use a specific and separate data repository, but there are still services that scholarly communication librarians can provide rather easily and that fit into the scope of existing services such as the mechanics of metadata creation and deposit for publications.

A NOTE ON SUPPORTING DATA

Often, the data which supports a particular article represents only a portion of the entire dataset collected by the scientist and his/her team. These cross sections or "slices" of the data might be termed supplemental, supporting, or article-level data given that they are narrowly associated with a particular research output or paper. This is an important distinction since it is more likely that the larger, raw datasets from which these supplements are derived will potentially yield future benefits to unknown future scholars and therefore require most careful documentation and preservation.

DESCRIPTIVE METADATA

After satisfying mandates to share their data, the most desirable outcome for scientists comes in having one's data cited. Ensuring discoverability of a scientist's datasets is the ultimate payoff for taking steps to document and preserve data. Librarians can make use of a variety of services to facilitate discovery and reuse of their organization's scientific datasets. All require consistent and accurate metadata and are most effective when standard identifiers are incorporated. Data that is well documented and curated is more likely to be cited, and perhaps citations to one's data (the true work in scientific research) will one day carry more weight than citations to one's papers (Pool, 2016; Coates, 2014).

The standard citation and tracking of datasets have drawn interest only in recent years, and consequently, there is variability both in how data is cited and which metadata elements should be included in a standard dataset citation. The absence of standard metadata for datasets is a challenge that librarians are helping to solve. Bibliographic data has had common elements recognized among publishers and libraries for years, but a standard set of terms to describe datasets does not share the same tradition

(Zotero, 2017). Unfortunately, many reference-management software applications today either do not include the reference type required to distinguish an item as a dataset or lack adequate metadata fields for description. But this may change as emphasis on sharing, citing, and archiving datasets increases.

DataCite (2017) is a membership organization with the goal of helping the research community locate, identify, and cite research data with confidence. Their website contains a list including the required creator/author, title, publication date, and identifier. To improve or enhance findability, elements such as resource type (e.g., tabular data, audio files, etc.), abstract or description, funding or award information are recommended. Science librarians should also review the Digital Curation Center website on How to Cite Datasets and Link to Publications[2].

One thing that facilitates the formal registration and subsequent citation of datasets is the use of digital object identifiers (DOIs). The creation of a stable identifier that provides unbreakable links to digital materials is key to the persistent access to datasets. This is a service that most institutional repository managers can provide if they become members of a DOI-creation agency like CrossRef or DataCite. Assigning DOIs to datasets forces the data creator or the librarian to think about metadata elements to describe the data, an exercise that will likely become easier through repetition.

The use of unique identifiers for datasets may allow for the standard collection of views, downloads, and/or citation counts for a particular dataset, and several parties are currently involved in making this happen. DataCite is working to incorporate datasets into community-recognized standards so that a citation can be easily identified as a dataset. They issue DOIs for datasets, support enhanced search and discovery, and are an advocacy group for standardizing data-citation practices. Science librarians who work in data-management services should be aware of DataCite and similar organizations in order to advise scientists and research information managers on best practices for ensuring that datasets are found, shared, cited, and, most importantly, included in research evaluation and metrics.

Clarivate Analytics (formerly part of Thomson Reuters) has developed the Data Citation Index in the same way that they have provided publication citation information via products such as the Web of Science. The fact that this long-time library vendor has launched a product like the

---

[2] http://www.dcc.ac.uk/resources/how-guides/cite-datasets.

Data Citation Index is an indication to science librarians that RDM is an area in which they should become involved. It is important for data creators to ensure that their materials are included in efforts such as the Data Citation Index, and science librarians are familiar enough with standard practices to help out in this effort.

There are emerging services that allow a search across research data repositories to find relevant datasets. For example, the DataMed.org, DataCite, and other sites include metadata about datasets from multiple repositories. Just as ensuring an organization's reprint repository is indexed by Google Scholar, getting scientific datasets included in federated search tools would be a core RDM service and one that many science librarians have an aptitude to provide. However, efforts to get particular scientific datasets included in aggregator services should only be done after ensuring that descriptive metadata is complete and accurate.

The creation of ORCIDs by an organization's researchers has benefits noted elsewhere, but one of them is the inclusion of datasets in a scientist's portfolio of works. Not only publications but datasets from standard repositories now include ORCIDs and allow the organization to pull metadata in order to populate a scientist's profile. Librarians can facilitate this in a number of ways, the most basic of which is to simply encourage scientists to register and use their ORCID whenever an online system requests it.

DATA DESCRIPTION

In addition to a description of the dataset (creator, date, sponsoring organization, etc.) a data dictionary and/or a code book should be developed for each research project and accompany any files which are copied or shared with others (International Standards Organization, 2015). These documents define data elements such as units of measurement, abbreviations, the instruments, the calibration and configuration, etc.

Librarians may not understand and indeed would not be required to grasp the technical details in the data dictionary but already possess an understanding of the value of metadata consistency and clarity. Librarians can inform scientists of the importance of making this information available wherever the raw data is stored or transmitted since without the inclusion of these (and many other) details, the data may become unusable or worse, misinterpreted. It is important that the data be intelligible to potential future users and comparable to traditional library descriptions and cataloging practices, a data dictionary ensures this utility.

Basic dataset readme files should include the identities of the PIs or those who collected the data as well as when it was collected and why. There should also be descriptions of what is being measured or described and methods or assumptions used. When working with tabular research data, all columns should be defined in terms of the source of the data (e.g., sensor or observation, etc.) valid or allowed values, units of measure and elaboration on any abbreviations, etc. The Natural Environment Research Council and the US Geological Survey websites have robust resources for the creation of data dictionaries.

It is easy to conclude that much the background and supporting information regarding the data elements and definitions is contained in the methods section of the article which is supported by the data. But best practices dictate that the data and its description stay as closely connected as possible. Were the data to be downloaded independent of the article it supports, it may be unusable at some point in the future. In addition, the methods section may describe only the supplemental data, and not the whole dataset. Librarians can help to ensure that metadata, data dictionary, and the data itself stay together and educate scientists to this need.

Some in the data management and scholarly communication world might argue for embedding metadata into data files so that there is no chance that the file and its description will be separated. Absent any accompanying description, the dataset will be nearly useless. Some formats and applications, particularly images and PDF and the Adobe suite of products, allow for embedded metadata, and while this is an ideal standard, it is sometimes not practical especially for busy scientists for whom the world of data management and sharing is new.

FILE NAMING, FORMATS, AND BACKUP

Further hands-on work with data-management services may eventually involve handling, transfer, and storage of the files. Despite excellence in their chosen field, some scientists do not (or cannot) devote much time to the naming and organization of files that make up their research data. However librarians know enough to take steps to ensure usability in their collections (whether print or digital), and among the things they look out for is the inadvertent separation of an item from its parent or container element. That's why most articles have a running journal title and enumeration on each page.

Similar considerations should be applied to the many files that can be generated by a research project. Not only for citation purposes and provenance do we need to know from where a particular piece of data came but proper file naming can augment data management by including administrative as well as descriptive elements. Certainly, a date in the form of YYYYMMDD is important in many (though not necessarily all) file-naming schema. Project name or collaborating unit (or agreed-upon abbreviations) are likewise very useful for data produced by a scientists involved in multiple projects and/or with external data contributors.

Where subsets of the data have to be quickly located, a well thought out file and folder hierarchy is critical. This is where librarians' expertise can be valuable. Organizing dozens or hundreds of files into folders representing dates, location, or equipment which generated the data is something that a library-run data-management service can help to ensure from the start and can payoff when it comes to sharing, reuse, and (ultimately) citations to the dataset.

The consistent naming of files which follows a certain convention is good data-management practice, and the use of a bulk file renaming tool is helpful. There is low-cost or free desktop software available to do this. In addition, librarians who are old enough to remember MS-DOS or who know other command-line systems may want to relearn the features of batch files or the creation of other commands that perform operations across large numbers of files. But even short of being directly involved, science librarians can always offer advice on consistent file naming, best practices, and related conventions for a given discipline.

It is likely that hands-on assistance with research data will involve the movement and renaming of large numbers of files, each of which may be of a size that typical library work has so far not encountered. These files may have to be moved in a method other than email attachment or simple copy from one drive to another; therefore, a facility with the use of file transfer protocol (FTP) client software or a service like DropBox is essential if the librarian becomes involved in this aspect of data management.

Scientific datasets come in many formats some of which may be unfamiliar to librarians. Some data may be in Microsoft Office (Office) formats such as Excel but sooner or later librarians working in data management will likely come across ASCII-formatted files. These are often delimited columns and rows in a generic format which can be imported into spreadsheets or databases for use by others. Delimiters used may be commas, tabs, the vertical pipe, or other special characters, and whichever is used, this should be documented. Files may alternatively be in XML format, and it is useful for science librarians offering data-management services to familiarize themselves with the concepts of XML. It is not necessary to become a proficient coder but only to develop a grasp of the concepts of XML and structured data using markup tags. Data files may occasionally need to be opened and viewed to verify and identify contents, and there are free software applications which have features such as color coding and indenting which makes it easier to read ASCII and/or XML files. Librarians providing RDM services should by all means become accustomed to opening and viewing data files using non-Office applications.

Science librarians working with tabular data may also see some benefit from investigating OpenRefine. Where legacy data exists in tabular or delimited format, this freely available package can cleanup and standardize the data, identifying inconsistent column names or other formats, and offer suggestions for replacement using a single click. There are many free resources including videos on using OpenRefine.

Other potential file formats may include software code, scripts, images, video, and audio, the latter two of which may be quite large. Each format has a specific three-digit extension which should be retained, and any repository deposit should contain descriptions of these files, at the very least their known formats. Some data repositories may not accept files except for a small number of known formats, and this is something about which library staff can investigate, document, and advise scientists.

DATA REUSE AND METRICS

The citation of articles by subsequent researchers may be well documented, but the reuse and citation of research data is still inconsistently tracked. However, there are some things librarians can do to track the reuse or reference to datasets. Until the infrastructure reaches that of the traditional article citation indexes that we are all familiar with, librarians can create alerts based on DOIs or use other informal methods of tracking data which are cited in subsequent papers. Implementing at least some of the practices outlined here and in other data curation resources is the key to realizing the benefits of research data sharing since the consistent citation of datasets will undoubtedly be accompanied by increased dissemination (Pasquetto et al., 2017)

PRESERVATION

Managing, sharing, and archiving data will inevitably foster a need for preservation. It is sometimes decided that certain research datasets should be retained indefinitely, while others have specific retention and disposition schedules. In cases where datasets are intended for long term or open-ended archiving, at least some attention and effort should be directed toward preservation. Many research institutions are still uncertain about what digital preservation will require, and efforts in this area are in the early stages. However, science libraries can serve as advisor to scientists on some known issues such as viability of file formats (e.g., proprietary versus open), media refresh and migration, and of course on metadata/documentation written with the aim of assisting future use or recovery of the data. We know that future researchers will likely have different hardware and software than we do now, so anything we can do to ensure that digital materials today are in as generic a format as possible might go a long way to extending the life of the files.

When their data is archived, it is common for scientists to expect that it will be archived in perpetuity. No matter the content, many will feel that if it's worth saving, it's worth saving forever. It is therefore helpful if the library staff who provide the service and assistance can articulate a more reasonable approach to managing the data. Like most people, scientists feel that their work is important, and even if it is not recognized so much today, there may come a time when future scientists discover that the tedious hours spent by previous researchers were not in vain and that their data will find a place in the scientific record.

Librarians know better than anyone the costs of managing collection objects beyond the acquisition price. It is often said the costs to catalog, label, barcode, handle, shelve, and shift a book exceeds its purchase price. This can be enlightening to scientists. It may be a delicate conversation, but all parties should be made aware that it is unrealistic to expect to keep everything forever. Many people feel that the primary cost to keeping digital collections lies in storage. And despite the cost of storage declining quickly (at least at the retail level), many fail to recognize the costs of metadata management, cleanup, integration with a growing list of external services, identifier registration, and other matters. Storage of research data also implies maintaining backups, redundancy, offsite storage, periodic data refresh, and verification of file readability, etc. all of which incur costs. In addition, dealing with multiple datasets from different labs means that different standards must be used or the various projects must be retrofitted into the existing repository and metadata model being used. The inevitable errors in data, customer service requirements, documentation, and other administrative tasks ultimately mean that the cost of archiving and making research datasets available is far more than the cost of disk storage.

DATA AS PRIMARY RESEARCH OUTPUT

When we consider the accomplishments regarding text and data mining, particularly in the field of journalism, it is not difficult to think that one day a machine will be able to read a dataset and generate hypotheses or intelligible prose based on the data and its description, methods, and other contextual information. The interpretation of raw data into human-readable language is already being done to some degree by companies with some facility in artificial intelligence. It is likely that this technology will advance and become more refined, affordable, and user-friendly so that one day scientific research data can be mined for suggested findings, trends, models, and other results that otherwise may take weeks or months to conclude. Developments in this area of data mining and natural language processing may mean that articles can be generated semiautomatically with the result being a greater emphasis on the data and its collection and documentation than on creating as many published papers as possible (Hutchinson, 2018).

If the scientific papers that result from tedious data collection are generated semiautomatically, this may circumvent what appears to be a common reason for reluctance that researchers express about sharing their data. They would (understandably) like to publish findings from the research data they worked so hard to collect. And as long as the scientific paper is the standard by which researchers are evaluated, the reluctance to share until they have the chance to fully realize the potential for publishing their results will probably remain. But if citation to one's data becomes as valuable to research evaluation, tenure, and review, etc. as having a paper published in *Science* or *Nature*, then it may be easier for a scientist to release their data to their peers for reuse.

Data-management services are highly variable and changing rapidly as tools, standards, and practices emerge. It is becoming one of the most recognizable services outside of traditional literature collection and retrieval that make science librarians more and more indispensable. Science librarians who keep abreast of developments in scientific research methods, data science, and related areas may find themselves invaluable to their organization. It does not require an advanced degree in a scientific discipline. Several blogs, listservs, and other social media channels cover recent innovation in these areas in layperson terms, and the creative application of this knowledge to one's home institution can reap many rewards for the librarian involved in RDM.

REFERENCES

Coates, H., 2014. Building data services from the ground up: strategies and resources. J. eScience Librarianship 3 (1), 52—59. Available from: https://doi.org/10.7191/jeslib.2014.1063.

DataCite, 2017. DataCite—Mission. Retrieved from: <https://www.datacite.org/mission.html> (accessed 19.04.17).

Hutchinson, A., 2018. Robotics Takes On Scientific Publishing—Digital Science Blog. Retrieved from: <https://www.digital-science.com/blog/guest/robotics-takes-on-scientific-publishing/> (accessed 27.04.18).

International Standards Organization, 2015. Information Technology—Metadata Registries (MDR)—Part 1: Framework. <https://www.iso.org/obp/ui/#iso:std:iso-iec:11179:-1:ed-3:v1:en>.

Pasquetto, I.V., Randles, B.M., Borgman, C.L., 2017. On the reuse of scientific data. Data Sci. J. 16 (8). Available from: https://doi.org/10.5334/dsj-2017-008.

Pool, R., 2016. "Dare to Share?" Research Information, December/January 2016—2017. <https://www.researchinformation.info/feature/dare-share>.

Zotero, 2017. Dev:translators:datasets [Zotero Documentation]. <https://www.zotero.org/support/dev/translators/datasets> (accessed April 14).

CHAPTER 8

Metrics and Research Impact

Increasingly, research organizations' budget allocations are influenced by research assessment, and a core component of that is bibliometrics (Åström and Hansson, 2013). This is also reflected on a national level as we see in the United Kingdom (Research Excellence Framework) and several other countries. Absent any evidence of research quality or impact, it becomes difficult to defend research budgets as governments become more cost-conscious (Brown, 2009). Upper level management of research organizations are also increasingly interested in measuring research output in several dimensions. Management sometimes wants to compare their organization to another for various reasons, vanity perhaps being among them. Likewise, there is often an interest in evaluating individual researchers or their departments as a regular exercise, in some cases as part of a formal review, accreditation, or tenure process. Beyond its use in rating or ranking, metrics can also analyze the research strengths of an organization; identify where research investment has the highest return; and create a narrative about research happening at the organization.

If ever there is a justification for librarians to develop metrics services, it is this recent emphasis on demonstrating the value of research investment. The growth of bibliometric services in libraries is well documented, often in response to performance-based funding both at the national and organizational level (Bladek, 2014). As with most new service development in science libraries, the groups that benefit from metrics exercises often are those that have not typically used the library. Primary among them is institutional administration which has been identified as an important user group of bibliometrics (Corrall et al., 2013).

LIBRARIAN INVOLVEMENT: REASONS AND RELUCTANCE

Like other service development, metrics and impact evaluation are opportunities which science librarians have been exploring in response to the increasing independence of patrons and the self-service nature of their libraries (Åström and Hansson, 2013). The expansion of services to a nontraditional user base can open up a range of services once there is

Science Libraries in the Self-Service Age
DOI: https://doi.org/10.1016/B978-0-08-102033-3.00008-8

recognition of library competencies beyond building, maintaining, and providing access to collections and literature.

Librarians generally have a trustworthiness within their organizations and have access to the publications and the tools to provide support in this area. Familiarity with scholarly publishing, bibliographic metadata, and related tools aside, another good reason for libraries to become involved in bibliometric services is their neutral position in most organizations where other units may be the subject of bias or at least suspicions. This impartiality allows libraries to remain aloof from local cultures which may bias review and evaluation processes (Brown, 2009). The relative goodwill and impartiality at their home organization may be flattering, but most librarians are reluctant to be seen as evaluating scholars or identifying those that are somehow underachieving (Åström and Hansson, 2013).

Despite being well positioned to participate in research metrics activities, many librarians may lack the skills to perform with confidence—at least initially. While it may be a stereotype, librarianship continues to draw people primarily trained in the humanities where training opportunities for data manipulation might not be available or emphasized. Further, statistical analysis may not be a strength of some librarians and therefore present an obstacle to his/her involvement with this kind of service. For example, it may be difficult to explain the significance or difference between scores such as h–index, impact factor (IF), Eigenfactor, etc. Lack of skills and confidence in interpreting and manipulating data has been cited as perhaps the biggest barrier to establishing bibliometric services in the past (Corrall et al., 2013). Along with a lack of formal training in library and information science (LIS) degree programs, this has meant that much of the existing knowledge of bibliometrics among librarians is self-taught or takes place on the job (Haddow and Mamtora, 2017; Zhao, 2011)

METADATA COLLECTION

Where librarians become involved in individual or institutional research metrics, a collection of data on research outputs—particularly peer-reviewed publications—is a critical resource for building a comprehensive service. There are commercial vendors with whom most science librarians are familiar and who aggregate scientific publications and provide citation data. However, bibliographic data corresponding an institution's research output is increasingly available with low investment of resources due to the use of standard formats and identifiers in the digital era of scientific publishing. Alongside the growing availability of article-level data, many associated services have become available ensuring that data collection can be leveraged in many ways ensuring the librarians that indispensability to the parent organization will increase.

Even where there is not a formal collection of metadata by librarians, several library vendors now provide services to meet this need. Major indexes to scientific literature now include citation counts, organizational identifiers, and other tools to enable the creation of reports and numeric scores for publications, their authors, and their institutions. The inevitable move toward a self-service model in research metrics gathering and the possibilities for misinterpretation or abuse of the data mean that it is imperative for library services in this area to include education of all users about these issues before they are removed from the process entirely.

CAVEATS AND USER EDUCATION

It is important for librarians who become involved in metrics services to learn about and then remind users of issues around the responsible use of metrics. Initial discussion between librarians and scientists should begin with a number of caveats including assumptions about objectivity and numeric scores that many researchers may adhere to. For example, publication and citation patterns differ between disciplines—even within the sciences—and this should be factored into metrics which are used for research-evaluation purposes. It may be helpful to point out that peer review is also an inexact process with sometimes unconscious biases and other subjective qualities (Belter, 2017). In any case, it is best to recommend bibliometrics be used as part of a larger evaluation process which includes some qualitative component (European Commission, 2017).

Just as commercial bibliometrics services are becoming mature (and reaching a self-service model), there is growing disillusionment with traditional measurements of research quality. Nowhere is this more evident than in the San Francisco Declaration on Research Assessment (DORA). This grassroots effort of mostly scientific research organizations and individuals issued a statement in 2012 which "recognizes the need to improve the ways in which the outputs of scientific research are evaluated" and has been signed by over 800 organizations and 12,000 individuals (DORA, n.d.). The main point of this and other objections to commonly accepted bibliometric methods for research evaluation is that they perpetuate perverse incentives which often do not adequately recognize or reward innovation or efforts to modernize scientific communication (European Commission, 2017). In addition, increasing emphasis on research metrics contributes to what many see as an audit culture in research organizations.

Another major event in the development of standard metrics criticism is the Leiden Manifesto published in 2015. It emphasizes 10 principles to guide research metrics including recommendations to use both qualitative and quantitative measures; transparent methods; and to account for variations in different disciplines, among other things. Science librarians can at the very least keep their user communities informed of these and related issues.

SERVICE DEVELOPMENT AND PLANNING

As with all service development in research libraries, with metrics services there is a tendency to start small and start right away. This can be effective and is most practical given resource constraints and uncertainty around the capacity to support a larger suite of services. But eventually if the service grows to become more popular, it will benefit (or will have benefitted) from formal planning. This includes identifying target audiences, creating a communication strategy, and defining the service.

Raising awareness of the tools available, the standard measures, and importantly, the potential for misuse is one service that does not require a great deal of investment and can potentially lead to more hands-on work. The creation of resource guides and/or web pages describing bibliometric and other tools and measures could be valuable to a research organization. Training and in-person presentations, particularly to groups which are involved in research-evaluation programs, can also be quick wins in this kind of service development. None of these demand an in-depth knowledge of statistics or skills in data manipulation.

Similarly, objections to research-evaluation methods may be outside of the librarian's expertise, but the issues can be highlighted in communication efforts. Information literacy might be supplemented by a "bibliometric literacy" to prevent misuse or misapplication of this kind of data. Certainly those being measured (scientists) would appreciate the impartiality of their librarian in the process. But whatever be the level of support for bibliometric service in libraries, it has to start with an in-house awareness of the issues and staff who can devote time to learning them.

However, metrics exercises need not concern themselves only with research ranking and impact or evaluation. Metrics can demonstrate areas of research activity or areas where research activity has been lacking. Likewise, librarian–led metrics exercises need not be limited to the home institution. Evaluating activity at similar institutions can be useful, not necessarily as a comparison of advantage or disadvantage in accomplishments but in demonstrating where research strengths are and where collaboration may be possible.

Eventually, the science librarian may become involved in the collection and reporting of data used in research metrics, and that is where the mention of caveats and controversies in the previously mentioned guides, training, and presentations might be of value.

BIBLIOMETRICS

Bibliometrics, the count of publications and citations to those works, has its origins in scientific inquiry. Eugene Garfield, considered the father of citation metrics, studied chemistry and linguistics and was the founder of the Institute for Scientific Information. The Journal IF (JIF), which he first developed, was originally used as a collection development tool for librarians and a proxy for journal quality. The JIF eventually became the gold standard for research evaluation whereby getting your paper accepted to a journal with a high IF as considered a key accomplishment. Bibliometrics has since been quantitative in nature with numeric scores used in comparative evaluation.

Two basic flavors of bibliometrics are the number of publications by a person, department, or organization and the number of times those publications are cited by others. Citation counts are normally obtained via three commonly used online tools: the commercially licensed, Web of Science and Scopus, and the freely available Google Scholar. However, due to publishing and other bibliographic anomalies, searching for an individual, an institution, and even a journal title across these three can often yield different results, calling the process into question.

Bibliometrics, while it may be used primarily for the evaluation of a researcher, department, or entire organization, has other applications in fostering research productivity and effectiveness. The identification of gaps in areas of research can be the result of the bibliometric analysis of an organization's publication track record. A look at citations both backward and forward from a given set of publications can also help identify potential collaborators and future research projects.

According to "Next-Generation Metrics" (European Commission, 2017), bibliometrics can also be used to quantify collaborations based on coauthorship. The Leiden Ranking http://www.leidenranking.com/ may be worth looking into as a tool to identify interinstitutional collaboration which seems to be an area of increasing emphasis in research funding. As with all metrics, total collaborations should be calculated with other factors in mind such as the size of the institution (and therefore the number of research opportunities on which to collaborate), and the number of papers produced as publishing patterns vary among disciplines, and a high number of coauthored papers may not necessarily reflect a high number of collaborations. It should be noted that several of the standard bibliometrics tools which count citations also include author affiliations and can be used for a rough overview of collaborations for institutions which are not included the Leiden Ranking.

Bibliometrics includes an array of statistical indexes in addition to the JIF. Some of these scores measure different things—the individual, the paper, or the journal, for example—and this could be a hindrance where a librarian lacks familiarity with either the underlying data, the calculation, or the meaning of the number. In recent years, the development of statistical scores related to individual authors has many scientists pursuing and thinking about their score. The h-index is perhaps most widely known at this time, but there are others. Author-centric numeric scores often take a total number of published works, the total citations to those works, and more recently factor in the career length of the researcher to reach some measurement of research impact. As always, these tend to become controversial soon after they are introduced.

CITATION METRICS VERSUS IMPACT

Research impact is variously defined but can be summarized as having an effect, benefit, or contribution to economic, social, cultural, and other aspects of the lives of citizens and society beyond contributions to academic research (Barnes, 2015). Researchers may have a broad range of reasons for citing or otherwise interacting with a scientific publication. Formally mentioning another paper can have meaning besides being a supposed proxy for research quality. It is for this and other reasons that research evaluation has expanded into other forms of metrics and the assessment of research impact.

In recent years, there has been a less rigid method of measuring research outputs, specifically with regard to the influence of scientific research outside of academia. Measuring citations can be seen sometimes as a closed system, showing which scientists cited other scientists with little information about the broader reach of research. As funding agencies and research institutions have begun to focus more on the return on investment, the emphasis on impact of research has drawn more and more attention. An increasing emphasis on translational science may have some part in the popularity of measuring research impact beyond academia.

ALTMETRICS

Out of this desire to demonstrate impact has come altmetrics, among other things. Originally derived from the phrase "article-level metrics," altmetrics measure more immediate impact of published research including when the research was mentioned in social media, news media, policy documents, and such.

Altmetrics is defined by the National Information Standards Organization as "broad term that encapsulates the collection of multiple digital indicators related to scholarly work. These indicators are derived from activity and engagement among diverse stakeholders and scholarly outputs in the research ecosystem, including the public sphere" (NISO, 2016). Altmetrics depends on standard identifiers (digital object identifiers (DOIs), in the case of scientific articles) and the ability to capture when these identifiers are mentioned on other online platforms (e.g., blogs, Twitter, Wikipedia, Facebook, etc.).

Altmetrics differs from traditional research metrics in several ways among which two deserve the most emphasis: first is that data on altmetrics is available almost immediately after publication of an item online. Traditional bibliometrics are not measured until a time period sufficient to allow other scholars to formally cite the article being measured in subsequent works. The journal IF requires 2 years of citation data at least, but many complain that even that is too short a time period to evaluate the impact of an article. But with altmetrics and social media, the impact of a publication—while amorphous—is nonetheless identified almost immediately after its release online (and sometimes in prepublication).

The second point to emphasize is that altmetrics measures "attention" rather than "intention." That is, when online social media activity around a published work takes place, it is not clear what the person's interest is. It may be a fellow scientist who wants to spread the word about a particular paper or it could be a casual observer interested in the subject.[1] The only thing that can be learned from social media activity is that some individuals noticed the research and mentioned it to their sphere of cohorts. Citation of an article, on the other hand, shows clearly that an author used the a publication to further scientific research. For that reason, altmetrics is called qualitative and bibliometrics, quantitative.

The office of sponsored research is among the departments which are potential users of altmetric services as they can help to enhance grant applications by mentioning media attention to illustrate impact of an applicant's previous research. These narratives can demonstrate societal impacts and the return to taxpayers and funders. While this may be more difficult to quantify, an application that mentions references to both mainstream and social media attention being paid to the scientist's previously published research may improve the chances for getting the award. Science librarians who become involved in monitoring media attention of their researchers can work with offices of sponsored research or similar units to help educate grant applicants to include stories taken from media and other non-scholarly impact to potentially strengthen their applications.

This information can also be used to support storytelling for institutional communication efforts and fundraising purposes. An institutional membership with an altmetric aggregator or service allows greater leverage and selection of detail and appeals to a wider audience than just the scientist. The ability to identify bloggers and Twitter users who are interested in an organization's research may be valuable to a number of people. Social media participation can also help identify potential collaborators and inform future research projects since more and more scientists

---

[1] Interest is also generated by social media which is controlled by robots or other automated means or by those with perverse incentives (ridiculing where research dollars are spent, for example or those with an interest in the salacious as with a paper discussing the sexual behavior of certain organisms).

themselves generate social media activity including bookmarking, highlighting, tweeting, or blogging about research done by others.

Media mentions about individual papers is easily found on journal websites, but there are commercial services that aggregate this data to offer an overview of social media activity around all publications by an author or his/her institution. They require a collection of research outputs (preferably with DOIs) for which the vendors then aggregate associated social and other media attention. Altmetric.com and PlumX are two of the primary players in this space. (PlumX is owned by science publisher Elsevier, a further indication of the movement of these traditional library vendors into new service areas.) These and related altmetric services can be licensed but require some effort to aggregate institutional data, disambiguate authors and departments within the organization, etc. When launched, they offer a portal with methods of grouping or narrowing down metrics for different facets of the organization. The customized site is of course available to anyone in the institution on a self-serve basis, but as with most new online tools, adoption may be slow at first and the library staff may serve as intermediary.

The use of standard application programming interfaces (API) to redisplay altmetric data on an institutional web page is often available through subscription with a service provider and can go a long way to demonstrate impact and reach to the home organization's nonscientist community. Several offices beyond research groups will all find value in highlighting institutional research on their web pages, and facilitating the inclusion of this information is an easy win for librarians.

Altmetrics as an area of reliable statistical study is still in its early years. Whether it is statistically related to article citations may not be important given that the value of a piece of research may be entirely subjective. So "impact" may be more easily described using altmetrics to tell a story since it is a more subjective and nuanced idea. An inordinate amount of attention may be paid to research topics that are more accessible to the general public such as papers on human origins or animal sexual behavior as opposed to something like high-energy physics.

Doubts about the validity of altmetrics as a formal research-evaluation tool are common, and most consider the services to be supportive of the work done in offices such as media and communications or fundraising and development. There is also undoubtedly some remaining misunderstanding among scientists about their creation and use. Librarians who develop metrics services should anticipate residual skepticism and perhaps resistance by emphasizing the supplemental role that altmetrics play in research metrics and their primary appeal to those outside of formal review and evaluation groups.

OTHER METRICS

Somewhere between bibliometrics and altmetrics is what might be considered "usage" metrics (European Commission, 2017). This can include the number of views or downloads of a digital research object (such as a paper or dataset). Like the other metrics, usage may not create a full picture of the impact of a scholar or his/her work. Many works are viewed, downloaded, printed, and read without being formally cited. As with altmetrics, it is said that usage metrics measure attention rather than intention. Increasingly, journal publishers include download and view statistics on the article landing page. Most repository platforms include a statistics component although these are continually being enhanced and refined in response to user needs. Web crawlers and robots can skew numbers upward. A recent initiative by Jisc is IRUS-UK (Institutional Repository Usage Statistics) is meant to collect repository statistics based on the COUNTER model that many librarians are familiar with from eJournal usage metrics. Another initiative from Montana State University with the University of New Mexico, ARL and OCLC is Repository Analytics & Metrics Portal. This effort has similar intentions of standardizing repository usage statistics.

Also worth noting is that one of the indicators included in the commercial service, altmetric, is the number of Mendeley readers who have saved the item to their personal library. Mendeley (also owned by Elsevier) is a reference management tool with a social media component which makes it something of a blend between bibliometrics and altmetrics.

LIBRARY-MEDIATED VERSUS SELF-SERVICE METRICS TOOLS

One thing librarians should keep in mind about self-service and the licensing of online resources is that certain users will only help themselves so far. Searching and downloading or printing articles from publisher websites has caught on, but other more esoteric tools will require library mediation—at least until users become comfortable with them. At this time, this is particularly true with online metrics resources such as the

Journal Citation Reports, Altmetric for Institutions, PlumX, and others. The user interface may not be as familiar as Google Scholar, and it doesn't take much unfamiliarity to prompt a scientist that it is too much bother and that he or she has more pressing matters to attend to. This is likely true for the time being with another audience of metrics services: institutional administration.

This may be a mixed blessing in which it allows the science librarian to showcase his or her expertise and value to the organization—for a while, that is. Over time, the adoption of these more sophisticated library tools will become wider and wider. This is due both to the facility with the online world that younger scientists bring with them when they finish graduate school and to the inevitable improvements in user interface and experience. As with other digital library services, the proficiency of previously reluctant users with these tools generally advances to the point that it becomes a largely self-service resource.

ADDITIONAL TOOLS AND APPLICATIONS

The emergence of organizational, funding, and facility (e.g., laboratories or field station) identifiers that are agreed upon and shared among research institutions could likewise make a good deal of research reporting and metrics much easier. Science librarians should keep abreast of developments in the use of unique, persistent identifiers and think about ways where they can be applied to their own institution's research data. Many of the organizations which create and provide identifiers are also developing APIs for librarians and IT staff to use these services more uniformly and with less effort than manual use.

One thing that comes to mind most immediately in the discussion of bibliometrics is the evaluation of an individual scientist, his/her department, or organization. But bibliometrics has other applications. The evaluation of journal titles (based on citations to articles within them) can be useful for librarians in collection development. Journal metrics are also potentially useful to scientists when thinking about where to publish their papers. Although most scientists work in a discipline narrow enough for them to feel that they are familiar enough with the available journals to which they might submit a paper, a list of journal rankings from one of the standard services might be enlightening. Depending on interest, a list of journal rankings in a specific discipline may be warranted every 5 years not only for the science librarian but for researchers as well.

SUMMARY

The reduced library visits and need for personal contact by scientists have led to the development of different service areas by science librarians. An emphasis on return on research investment, translational science, and public impact of scientific research means that research metrics are becoming more and more recognized by librarians as a potential service to the organization. Citation databases are available for traditional bibliometrics, and alternative metrics are emerging as a desirable resource among non-research user communities. Librarians sometimes express reluctance to enter into this kind of service for a variety of reasons but merely educating the user community about the types of metrics, but also the potential for misuse is one type of activity that librarians are well positioned to offer. Their relative neutrality in most research organizations also makes librarians a natural choice for this kind of service.

The area of research metrics has gained a lot of attention in recent years, and the tools and measurements being developed are evolving quickly. Librarians offering support for metrics will need to keep up-to-date on these changes to allow this set of services to develop (Roemer and Borchardt, 2015 p. 214).

REFERENCES

Åström, F., Hansson, J., 2013. How implementation of bibliometric practice affects the role of academic libraries. J. Librarianship Inf. Sci. 45 (4), 316—322. Available from: https://doi.org/10.1177/0961000612456867.

Barnes, C., 2015. The use of altmetrics as a tool for measuring research impact. Austr. Acad. Res. Lib. 46 (2), 121—134. Available from: https://doi.org/10.1080/00048623.2014.1003174.

Belter, C.W., 2017. Talking to Researchers About Metrics. Retrieved from: <https://www.brighttalk.com/webcast/9995/257883/researcher-profiles-and-metrics-that-matter>.

Bladek, M., 2014. Bibliometrics services and the academic library: meeting the emerging needs of the campus community. Coll. Undergrad. Lib. 21 (3—4), 330—344. Available from: https://doi.org/10.1080/10691316.2014.929066.

Brown, S., 2009. A Comparative Review of Research Assessment Regimes in Five Countries and the Role of Libraries in the Research Assessment Process. OCLC Research, Dublin, OH.

Corrall, S., Kennan, M.A., Afzal, W., Wallace, D., Gandel, P., Cogburn, D., et al., 2013. Bibliometrics and research data management services: emerging trends in library support for research. Lib. Trends 61 (3), 636—674. Available from: http://doi.org/10.1353/lib.2013.0005.

DORA, 2012. San Francisco Declaration on Research Assessment. Retrieved from: <http://www.ascb.org/dora/>.

European Commission Expert Group on Altmetrics, 2017. Next-Generation Metrics: Responsible Metrics and Evaluation for Open Science, European Commission, Brussels.

Haddow, G., Mamtora, J., 2017. Research support in Australian academic libraries: services, resources, and relationships. New Rev. Acad. Librarianship 23 (2−3), 89−109. Available from: https://doi.org/10.1080/13614533.2017.1318765.

NISO, 2016. Outputs of the NISO Alternative Assessment Metrics Project. National Information Standards Organization, Baltimore, MD.

Roemer, R.C., Borchardt, R., 2015. Meaningful Metrics: A 21st Century Librarian's Guide to Bibliometrics, Altmetrics, and Research Impact. ASSN Coll & Research Lib, Chicago, IL.

Zhao, D., 2011. Bibliometrics and LIS education: how do they fit together? Proc. Am. Soc. Inf. Sci. Technol. 48 (1), 1−4. Available from: https://doi.org/10.1002/meet.2011.14504801190.

PART II

Cost Savings as a Service

Academic libraries that fail to demonstrate their value, that fail to align their priorities to the goals and objectives of their host institutions, face possible extinction

Maxwell (2016)

Science libraries are beginning to see a need to expand their user base in order to ensure wider support within their home organization. Many of the services discussed in this book are proof that libraries can show their importance to the research enterprise outside of traditional acquisition, reference, and circulation of print publications. However, the value that libraries bring to their parent organization can be defined more broadly than service to scientists. Many nonscientists who work at research organizations are the targets of innovative library services that have been implemented in recent years.

Among the institutional groups which have benefitted from new ways of doing business in science libraries are people in the upper management and administration of the organization (Corrall et al., 2013). As discussed elsewhere, librarians have initiated scholarly communication services which provide management with reports on research outputs and metrics. But librarians can and should also consider this group's other goals: budget, finance, and cost control.

With libraries required to add value to the parent organization, it is important to demonstrate that value can be delivered in as many ways as possible including those that are more subtle and perhaps not apparent to those who think of libraries in the traditional sense. When the work of scientists is supported by library services, it is easy to recognize the value that provides. But traditional services on which scientists depend must be delivered at a sustainable cost as far as the organization's administration is concerned. The judicious use of scarce resources like materials funds and physical space can provide tangible benefits to the institution's administration, many of whom may never borrow a book or use library-licensed digital materials.

Certainly in the last few decades, the development of scan-and-send technology as well as the licensing of online content have had implications for more efficient service delivery. They allow the user to remain in his/her office or lab and also offer more precise data on which resources and services are used most. The product (an article in the hands of a reader) is the same as it's ever been, but with some savings realized.

Where print subscriptions are canceled in favor of electronic licensing, the processing workflow changes presumably toward greater value to the research institution. It should be noted that simply shifting from print to digital may not represent a tremendous cost savings for the library. Digital materials don't need to be reshelved or occupy a central place on campus but hardware, software, and (until a universal interface is ubiquitous) training must accompany the licensing or acquisition of digital content. But when reader convenience and reduced space needs are considered, the licensing of electronic content likely presents some resource savings on balance for the institution—particularly with journals where handling costs are high and adoption of electronic formats is nearly universal.

Where print articles are scanned and delivered to a scientist, it is true that the citation still has to be identified in the collection, retrieved, scanned, and sent. But where this is performed by library technicians rather than scientists, the organization will certainly recognize some cost efficiency. This kind of cost-accounting may be repulsive to some library staff but when it becomes clear for whom the organization exists, it is sensible to show the benefit to the organization of the shift in staff duties which frees up the scientist's time.

Some of the steps that science libraries can take to deliver operational efficiency to their organizations' management are demand-driven acquisitions, reduced need for collections space, and the provision of library services with fewer staff. The recognition that only a fraction of research library materials are used immediately (or ever) is common knowledge among librarians, but were this to become widely known by institutional administration, it would likely be unsettling at least and untenable at most. Science librarians should anticipate the recognition by the organization of declining use of physical collections and space by planning for eventual space reconfiguration and movement of print materials to remote storage (or their withdrawal).

Exercises in cost savings will undoubtedly be new to most librarians and will entail some trial and error where some innovation will be met with resistance or have to be abandoned for other reasons. The important thing is to show that you recognize the near-continuous squeeze on the finances of nonprofit (and even some for profit) research enterprises and that the library is willing to make sacrifices. The good news is that automation can help ameliorate what would otherwise be a notable reduction in level of service and that libraries are most apt to implement IT solutions aimed at operational efficiency.

Sadly, in the business world and increasingly in nonprofits, staff are viewed as costs that might be more efficiently deployed or cut altogether. In libraries, we see more professional staff taking on the duties previously done by professional librarians. As certain skills—especially information technology skills—become more widespread and command less of a salary premium, it is tempting to hire nonlibrarians to perform more and more functions (Neal, 2006). It has been demonstrated in some research libraries that a reference desk (where it hasn't been eliminated entirely) is most cost effective when staffed by paraprofessional or generalist staff, referring more sophisticated queries to subject-specialist and other librarians with the required expertise (Sutton and Grant, 2011; Merkley, 2009).

It is important for science librarians to illustrate both successful cost savings and to good faith efforts to rein in spending when reporting on activities to organizational administration. Not all changes in operations go as planned and others may not come to fruition. But leadership must be reminded that the library is continually looking for ways to economize in collections and services. Libraries have a tradition of goodwill among many parties in a research organization and they should leverage that goodwill to navigate the changes that digital information have brought (Lewis, 2007).

The following chapters are intended to illustrate two core examples of how science libraries are meeting the need to operate a robust suite of services on flat or reduced budgets. Creative science librarians will undoubtedly think of more ways to make their processes more efficient and it will be wise to alert upper management to these innovations.

REFERENCES

Corrall, S., Kennan, M.A., Afzal, W., Wallace, D., Gandel, P., Cogburn, D., et al., 2013. Bibliometrics and research data management services: emerging trends in library support for research. Libr. Trends 61 (3), 636–674. Available from: https://doi.org/10.1353/lib.2013.0005.

Lewis, D.W., 2007. A strategy for academic libraries in the first quarter of the 21st century. Coll. Res. Libr. 68 (5), 418–434.

Maxwell, D., 2016. The research lifecycle as a strategic roadmap. J. Libr. Adm. 56 (2), 111—123. Available from: https://doi.org/10.1080/01930826.2015.1105041.

Merkley, C., 2009. Staffing an academic reference desk with librarians is not cost-effective. Evid. Based Libr. Inf. Pract. Available from: https://doi.org/10.18438/B89S40.

Neal, J.G., 2006. Raised by Wolves: integrating the new generation of feral professionals into the academic library. Libr. J. 131, 41—44.

Sutton, A., Grant, M.J., 2011. Cost-effective ways of delivering enquiry services: a rapid review. Health Inf. Libr. J. 28 (4), 249—255. Available from: https://doi.org/10.1111/j.1471-1842.2011.00965.x.

CHAPTER 9

Purchase-On-Demand Services

[W]e should always be looking for ways to do what we do more cheaply as well as better, because if we can do some things more cheaply (holding quality constant) it enables us to do everything better, including improving quality.

Courant (2008)

NOTE: Much of this chapter assumes that the commercial subscription-based journal model will coexist with open-access (OA) journal content—at least for a while. However, it should be noted that an effort such as OA2020 (https://oa2020.org/) suggests that perhaps all subscription-based content can be "flipped" to OA availability by diverting library journal acquisitions funds to pay author OA processing fees. In that case, some of the article-purchasing services suggested in this chapter may lose their relevance. Time will tell.

OPERATIONAL EFFICIENCY AS A SERVICE

Among the many ways that librarians support their research organizations, one that is often overlooked is the more efficient delivery of existing services. This form of support may not be noticeable to most because it does not involve new services or products but rather the delivery of the same service at a lower cost. The recipients of this kind of service are not traditional library readers but rather the institutional administration since they ultimately benefit from reduced resource needs of the library. Increasing efficiency brings value to the parent organization in the same way that a newly introduced service might.

ACQUISITIONS AND OTHER COSTS

Because salaries and benefits of library staff are costs that are largely inherited and static, one of the most easily recognized costs associated with library operations is in the acquisition and licensing of collections resources. Traditionally, science libraries (indeed almost all research libraries) have purchased materials based on a decision by a collection-development librarian as

Science Libraries in the Self-Service Age
DOI: https://doi.org/10.1016/B978-0-08-102033-3.00009-X

to whether the items are within the scope of the library and whether s/he feels that the item will be useful to future patrons. This may have worked well when the volume of published material was smaller, but in recent years, the scholarly output in the sciences has increased beyond libraries' capacity to keep up.

When considering that many library acquisitions budgets are flat, the increase in published output means that librarians must be more selective in collection development. Particularly in the sciences where journal prices have increased well beyond the rate of inflation and expanded much faster than typical library budgets, acquisition of funds has slowly shifted from monographs to serials over the past few decades to cover these increases. The traditional model of buying books based solely on its subject matter and collection scope is one of the casualties of this new economic reality. In addition, many studies show circulation statistics are declining in research libraries and because the core literature of most sciences lies in journal articles rather than books, many science librarians are understandably hesitant to spend money on books unless there is a clearly stated need.

TOTAL COST OF OWNERSHIP

Despite these enormous budget pressures, some feel that comprehensive library collections should be built in a specific subject regardless of the cost. This often comes from a nostalgic view of libraries that "have everything" and where library value is based on size. Besides the unfortunate unsustainability of this philosophy (outside of the most well-endowed libraries), it should also be noted that the "cost" of a library book is often far higher than commonly believed when considering the expense of not only purchase but of handling, cataloging, processing, and preserving, and this is often unrecognized by most librarians (Courant and Nielsen, 2010).

Costs of owning a single book may seem small but of course add up not only across a collection of thousands but also through years where the item (according to many studies) may never be used. Some may counter that although a particular title is purchased but does not circulate in 10–20 years, that doesn't mean that it is worthless. They may reasonably ask: Who knows what research needs will emerge in later decades that lead a scholar to an old book that garnered very little usage when it was published? Nonetheless, science librarians face budget pressures and need increasingly to demonstrate to their organizational administration their efforts at fiscal control, and new methods of managing their finances include new methods of library acquisitions.

In the latter decades of the 20th century, some academic librarians began to wonder whether purchasing materials based on speculation of what may one day be useful has resulted in large collections occupying large spaces often (in the case of many university libraries) on a prime piece of real estate. At the same time, some studies of library circulation records have shown that much of research library material is used rarely if at all. As the annual output of published material in the sciences has grown in recent years (Bornmann and Mutz, 2015) and science library acquisition budgets have struggled to keep up, librarians began to question the cost-effectiveness of the traditional acquisition model. This awareness has many librarians thinking of the total cost of ownership.

Many librarians have begun to realize that with increasingly limited resources and the fact that much scientific literature is online and available instantly (or deliverable within a day or two), a more efficient method would dictate that items could be purchased at the point of user need, rather than ahead of time. This has led to the purchase-on-demand model of materials acquisitions. Also known as demand-driven acquisition (DDA) or patron-driven acquisition (PDA), this is a new way of thinking about providing research literature to patrons. Traditionally, librarians may have developed collections by reviewing new books lists, publisher catalogs, and advertisements for recent books, sometimes supplementing their wish lists with requests for specific titles from users. While this may have helped build the selection librarian's expertise and knowledge of the publishing landscape of a certain discipline, it has by many measures turned out to be inefficient as is demonstrated by low-circulation counts documented in the literature. There is some disagreement as to whether circulation counts are indeed as low as they are asserted to be; however, economics and business principles (to which libraries are increasingly subject) would emphasize that materials in the aggregate would be less costly if purchased or acquired at the point of need, especially given dramatic reduction in the time it takes to deliver library materials.

By changing the acquisitions model of buying books and journals based on a proven and immediate need rather than an anticipated future need of researchers, it is possible that several line items in the library's budget can be brought under control. Many of us are first introduced to libraries as places where everything is "free." But beyond the price of library materials, the total cost is one thing that is largely overlooked by library users and even many librarians. Some may believe that the cost of a library book lies almost entirely in its purchase price whereas often that is half or less of the total cost of owning a book, given storage, cataloging, handling, and other costs associated with acquiring a library book. DDA is at this time a fairly new concept for large libraries, and it is not clear what the long-term consequences are, but one can assume that cataloging, processing, space, and other costs will be somewhat ameliorated if DDA is adopted to some extent.

JUST-IN-TIME VERSUS JUST-IN-CASE

Science librarians have heard recent calls to be more "entrepreneurial." This has a broad variety of meanings, one being to apply the efficiencies that were once limited to the private sector such as those used in manufacturing or cost accounting. Consequently, many in the library world have begun to look to the private sector to draw comparisons in operations and to perhaps apply some lessons. One famous business innovation with some application to libraries came from the Japanese. In the 1970s, automobile manufacturers in Japan implemented what is called a "just-in-time" system of managing materials, parts, components, and inventory. This method has several varieties but common to them all is the policy of waiting for an expressed need or order before assembling the materials needed to manufacture the car. This meant that storing and managing an inventory of parts and supplies—and the subsequent finished product—was kept to a minimum. The reduction in storage and other associated costs was not insignificant, and several industries soon caught onto this method of logistics and operations management (The Economist, 2009).

On-demand library acquisitions in science libraries mimic the "just-in-time" model. This is often contrasted with the "just-in-case" model of acquisitions where materials are acquired based on some anticipated future use. But it is clear that decisions to purchase materials have to be judiciously considered since many books in science libraries may be rarely (if ever) used (O'Neill and Gammon, 2014). In the same way, that many people today treat transportation (e.g., ride-sharing) as a service rather than as an asset (ownership of a vehicle), librarians must at least evaluate whether access to information is more efficient than outright ownership. DDA emphasizes what we do for people more than what we have for people.

UNEVEN COLLECTION DEVELOPMENT

Some respond to this efficiency argument that over time, the coverage of a particular science library collection will be increasingly skewed to represent the fleeting topics of scientific interest that have come and gone over the years (Tyler et al., 2014). The institutional priorities for library-collection development can only come from a librarian with longer term vision and not from following the immediate needs of library users, the thinking goes.

While there is not a lot of evidence comparing PDAs with librarian-selected titles, the few studies that do exist show that readers largely request books that are within the collection-development policy of the library. When comparing the titles which were selected by science library users versus those selected by collection-development librarians, one study showed that the librarians purchased nearly twice as many items as the library user. This may indicate that the selectors in science libraries have been a bit too aggressive in purchasing books and that some of the titles may end up in the group of books that according to some studies never circulate (Goedeken and Lawson, 2015; Bracke, 2010).

Among other librarians, concerns are that patrons will ask for materials for personal or recreational rather than professional reading (Tyler et al., 2014) or that patrons will ask for materials which the library already owns (but that the reader was unable to find in the catalog). Part of the implementation of any DDA program inevitably must address these possible scenarios.

BOOKS ON DEMAND

Because the most heavily used scientific research literature is the peer-reviewed journal article, some may think that applying this DDA to science books is a moot point. Because an increasing share of the science library's acquisition budget goes to journals, few science books are purchased and that therefore a real test of DDA would be with single article buying as a substitute for subscriptions. But it is the low level of monograph buying that may make a new DDA service ideal for testing. After all, a shrinking book budget means that each purchase must meet a higher and higher justification threshold, and there is no better justification than immediate need.

Requests to purchase print books can easily originate from an interlibrary loan (ILL) book request that triggers the decision to purchase. This mediation by library staff allows them the most control, and where there is hesitation by librarians to explore DDA, it may be best to limit the service to print materials at first, provided the item can be purchased, and delivered as fast (or faster) than via traditional ILL.

Further, guidelines for DDA criteria can be created so that ILL staff (if the science librarian is unable to review requests) can purchase books without requesting review by the collection-development librarian. Restrictions could be placed on publication date (within the last 5 years, for example), a price cap, classification in certain subject categories, availability from an online bookseller, and/or limited to items from certain scholarly publishers.

With print DDA, there are questions about special handling, for example, whether the item is cataloged. Because the scientist requested the book specifically, it may be best to apply a property stamp and circulate it directly to him/her on delivery. But of course, the library needs to maintain a record of the item (lest it be inadvertently purchased a second time) and a reminder that when the requesting scientist is done with the book, it needs to be fully cataloged, labeled, barcoded, etc. Perhaps a flag in the circulation record prompting library staff to ask about returning the book for full cataloging after a specified interval is appropriate. Alternatively, books purchased on demand might be cataloged on a rush basis.

Ebook DDA is implemented somewhat differently than for print. And because of the relatively slow adoption of ebooks by readers of scholarly literature, any evaluation of a DDA program which includes ebooks should recognize format preference and variability. This will undoubtedly change as scientific organizations see a growth in staff who were introduced to such technologies at an early age.

Many ebook DDA programs mean that the library catalog is loaded with records for ebooks for which the library will rent or purchase, based on user need. When users find an electronic book in the catalog and click on a link to view or download the item, the library is billed for the item. Sometimes, these charges are tiered according to the amount of content viewed or downloaded or the amount of time spent reading the book online. In that way, libraries can purchase (or license or rent, if you will) a book based on a clear user need. Vendors have developed several cost and purchase models for distribution of these books, and they will likely be standardized in the near future.

A popular criticism of ebook vendors among academic libraries is that coverage in the sciences is weak, and this is understandable given the narrow and highly specific appeal of many science publications. However, this drawback seems to be mitigated in recent years as ebook popularity increases. Particularly in fields such as computer science and engineering, ebook vendor coverage has widened in recent years. Formats (PDF versus ePub versus Mobi) and reader preferences, hardware, etc. area all considerations when evaluating ebook vendor programs for on-demand acquisitions.

ALTERNATIVE SOLUTIONS

Many ebook vendors now offer what is commonly called, "evidence-based acquisition" (EBA) packages. One common complaint about ebook adoption is the inability to selectively choose titles and the requirement to purchase full collections, only a fraction of which may ever be used. The hybrid EBA model may offer a workable compromise between the publisher and library interests which appear to be in conflict. The model not only guarantees some minimum revenue for the publisher but also allows the library to be more selective in the ebooks it purchases. After a period of time with access to a large collection, an analysis of usage over the period produces a list of ebooks which the library can purchase based on subjects used, etc. The initial annual subscription is often applied toward the purchase of these individual titles.

As mentioned earlier, science monographs are not nearly as popular as journal literature, and therefore this kind of program may not have the same participation level in highly specialized science libraries. But it is worth noting that publishers and vendors are experimenting with alternative models of content purchase and that they are sensitive to the need to be increasingly selective. Science librarians should keep an eye on developments in these kinds of distribution business models to make the best of their limited acquisition funds.

Whether an approval plan is in place or not, science librarians may be able to use reference-management software to easily present their user community with candidates for purchase. Capturing bibliographic data published online has never been easier, and it may be worthwhile for science librarians to collect new book information via Zotero or Mendeley or one of the other (paid or free) applications. At selected intervals or when a critical mass of new titles is compiled, the list can be copied, pasted, or printed in a human-readable citation style and included in an email to scientist-users, requesting their input on which titles to purchase. Depending on the volume of books and the number of users, the science librarian could even take the results and determine the most desired titles based on the number of "votes" by the user community. This is in essence turning over collection development to the library users and is probably currently done in one form or another at many science libraries. It may be instructive to the selecting librarian to see what his/her patrons would choose versus what he/she might have chosen if the exercise was not undertaken. This type of home-grown hybrid solution is one of the many gaps opened up by the move toward self-service that science librarians can fill.

ARTICLES ON DEMAND

Purchase on demand can be applied to journal literature given that many commercial publishers now sell articles individually (with various pricing models) in addition to selling subscriptions to entire journal volumes. If most journal articles purchased under the traditional subscription model are not immediately needed and if they can be reliably purchased after-the-fact, then it may make sense to buy them as-needed rather than wholesale with a subscription renewal. It should also be recognized that the OA movement may change library budgets considerably.

Purchase on demand seems less controversial with articles—the common currency of scientific publications—compared to ebooks where usage may rely on specialized devices or software. With journal-cancelation exercises, an annual occurrence in many science libraries, some librarians feel that low usage of certain titles may justify cancelation and subsequently, any desired articles purchased individually, at the point of need. Articles which are published in journals with an online presence can be often purchased, downloaded, or printed within minutes of an identified user need. Ejournal statistics are becoming more reliable and can indicate views and downloads, allowing librarians to make better decisions on the break-even point of subscribing versus purchasing content article-by-article.

Outside of traditional ILL (which has seen sharp reductions in turnaround time thanks to scan-and-send technology), article-on-demand services can be mediated or unmediated and the choice that science librarians make will depend on a number of factors. The total user population is a good primary consideration when deciding whether articles on demand are unmediated or reviewed by library staff. A relatively low proportion of users to library staff may mean that it is not too difficult for ILL or other staff to review and authorize purchase of articles. However, one can imagine the staff time required if the service is offered to a library-user community that numbers in the hundreds or thousands. Many science librarians choose to mediate requests in the initial phases of deploying an article-on-demand service since most are (understandably) wary of runaway journal requests which may not become apparent until the first invoices are received.

Articles on demand can be facilitated in a number of ways. The easiest and perhaps most administratively cumbersome is for the ILL or some other office to purchase with a credit card at the point of need. Many science publishers such as Wiley, Elsevier, etc. offer deposit accounts, and some offer volume discounts which librarians can use to purchase against (Brown, 2012).

At a small scale, ordering articles one at a time may be an adequate substitute for cancelation of just a few journal subscriptions. But as the volume of this activity grows and becomes more popular, it is best to automate at least some of the process. Several commercial services have emerged to meet this use case. Depending on functionality, volume, and user community, one of these services might be helpful.

Some, such as that available from ReadCube, require a dedicated desktop application or browser plugin to request and receive articles. ReadCube (a Digital Science company) is an elaborate piece of software with services including a reference-management component, suggestions for similar articles, an enhanced PDF viewer and annotation tool, and automatic capture of supplements and citing papers.

Because it is a dedicated application, the service requires the cooperation of publishers. ReadCube has agreements with several science publishers but not all, and although the list may be expanded as time goes on, coverage is in no way complete or comprehensive at this time. In addition, a separate application may be adopted by many users, but undoubtedly there will be some that will not or that will require assistance and ultimately seek help from library staff. The potential for user support required of library staff should be included in considering any library-specific application including the one used for DDAs.

Other services such as Get it Now from the Copyright Clearance Center are quick and seamless, offering a mediated and unmediated versions. This service offers access (at this time) to a much larger body of literature. Mediated service works with the popular ILLiad ILL software. But despite not requiring a separate application to use, accessing the service does often require some setup and user training.

Several article-on-demand services include a tiered pricing structure which may have incremental charges for viewing the article online, for printing it, or for downloading a PDF. Some commercial publishers display these options on the article-level web page.

Many studies show that DDA services are cost-effective when compared to ILL. Users do not seem to abuse the service, and although there is some duplication, it does not appear to be more than what is found in traditional ILL service (England et al., 2015) In many (though not all) cases, it has been demonstrated that using the pay-per-view model of acquiring articles can lead to cost savings (Brown, 2012). Not only does the scientist get the paper more quickly, but the purchase costs are lower.

There are of course alternative methods for researchers to gain access to peer-reviewed literature. Aside from rogue copies on individual websites or from pirated versions on illegal servers, there is ResearchGate, a scholarly network where scientists can (among other things) share their reprints either seamlessly or on demand via a request button. There is DeepDyve, a subscription-based service, marketed directly to users whereby individuals can gain access to scholarly articles to view/print and in some cases purchase.

OVERHEAD AND ADMINISTRATION COSTS

However, some additional costs are incurred with DDA depending on the method used to access the articles. For example, reconciling credit card payments or deposit account statements takes staff time. Initial efforts to identify download and usage of particular titles require staff resources, and although it appears to be a one-time effort, this can and should be done on a continual basis to evaluate the service. Reviewing usage statistics to identify excess or abuse of the service may also require some staff time—at least in the initial phase of the service.

Of course any effort at cost savings in an institutional setting should bear in mind the perverse incentives that often exist when a department or unit makes efforts to save resources. Unfortunately, this sometimes results in the central administration reducing the subsequent years' budget allocation for the unit since the assumption is that the existing or present funding level was too high. The implementation of cost-saving measures by the library can be communicated to upper level management and with luck, some other considerations might be negotiated when showing a good faith effort to economize.

All DDA services will likely require some training. Even where a specific software application is not required, patrons will inevitably be presented with new and unfamiliar screens to navigate when requesting a book or article. They will need guidance not only on how to order the item but also how long they should expect to wait for delivery, what to do if it is not delivered as expected, where to look on the screen for a link if a link resolver is used, etc.

There are several considerations when implementing a service to purchase articles on demand rather than subscription-based access to journal articles. Some of the local concerns have been addressed by the more popular article purchase services such as duplicated purchase and abuse by click-happy patrons. Commercial services often come with options for level of access including limiting the user to read-only, print and a full download, and save the full article. These are priced accordingly in a parallel manner to ebook licensing where short-term views are cheap or free and increasing levels of usage incur higher and higher costs until the item is purchased outright.

However, upon reflection and practical implementation of such services, there are some tricky questions to answer. The first might be, how do we ensure that we don't purchase the same article twice? Or is it cost-effective to prevent duplicate purchase of the same article (assuming a method of tracking and following these requests involves some staff effort)? Buying the same article twice may not seem likely given the extremely narrow focus of most researchers and the specificity of the literature that interests them. However, when it comes to articles in general science journals such as *Science* and *Nature*, it may be worthwhile to monitor multiple purchases.

Should librarians look for an OA copy of an article requested for purchase? Should the user be permitted to purchase without the librarian acting as intermediary, and if so, what backstop will be implemented to prevent excessive purchases, etc.?

PUBLISHING BUSINESS IMPLICATIONS

Another concern not for the individual organization but still valid is that were all libraries to go to purchasing journal articles "by-the-drink" rather than subscribing, this might put economic pressure on publishers and their journals, threatening the survival of the vehicles in which scientists must publish their works. In fact, this probably applies to monograph publishing as well. Absent any subsidies (as we often see in university presses), monograph publishers who expect to turn a profit on book sales may balk at certain book proposals once they understand that research libraries are beginning to purchase selectively rather than systematically. Academic publishers have relied on library sales for many years, and if the consumer changes his/her behavior, the producer clearly has to respond. It may be that fewer books are published.

Economic implications may be larger than the library profession. Put another way, the viability of commercial publishers may not seem to be the problem that librarians are concerned with; content affordability and efficient use of scarce acquisitions resources is the problem we are trying to solve. But this issue should nonetheless be ignored. Remember, researchers are also authors and are required by the terms of their employment to publish their findings. If the outlets in which their papers can be published begin to disappear due to dwindling subscriptions (a more predictable source of revenue than single article sales), we will have inadvertently created a problem for them and, consequently, ourselves.

REFERENCES

Bornmann, L., Mutz, R., 2015. Growth rates of modern science: a bibliometric analysis based on the number of publications and cited references. J. Assoc. Inf. Sci. Technol. 66 (11), 2215–2222. Available from: https://doi.org/10.1002/asi.23329.

Bracke, M.S., 2010. Science and technology books on demand: a decade of patron-driven collection development, Part 2 science and technology books on demand: a decade of patron-driven collection. Collect. Manage. 2679 (March 2014), 37–41ISSN: Available from: https://doi.org/10.1080/01462679.2010.486742.

Brown, H.L., 2012. Pay-per-view in interlibrary loan: a case study. J. Med. Lib. Assoc. 100 (2), 98–103. Available from: https://doi.org/10.3163/1536-5050.100.2.007.

Courant, P.N., 2008. The future of the library in the research university. No Brief Candle: Reconceiving Research Libraries for the 21st Century, pp. 21–27.

Courant, P.N., Nielsen, M., 2010. On the cost of keeping a book. The Idea of Order: Transforming Research Collections for 21st Century Scholarship, pp. 81–105. Retrieved from ⟨https://www.clir.org/pubs/reports/pub147⟩.

England, M.M., Weisbrod, L., Jarvis, C., 2015. Article delivery using ReadCube access: a report on use in five US libraries. Interlending Doc. Supply 43 (4), 189—198. Available from: https://doi.org/10.1108/ILDS-07-2015-0023.

Goedeken, E.A., Lawson, K., 2015. The past, present, and future of demand-driven acquisitions in academic libraries. Coll. Res. Lib. 76 (2), 205—221. Available from: https://doi.org/10.5860/crl.76.2.205.

Just in Time, 2009. The Economist. ⟨http://www.economist.com/node/13976392⟩.

O'Neill, E.T., Gammon, J.A., 2014. Consortial book circulation patterns: the OCLC-OhioLINK study consortial book circulation patterns: the OCLC-OhioLINK study. Coll. Res. Lib. 75 (6), 791—807.

Tyler, D.C., Melvin, J.C., Epp, M., Kreps, A.M., 2014. Don't fear the reader: librarian versus interlibrary loan demand-driven acquisition of print books at an academic library by relative collecting level and by library of congress classes and subclasses. Coll. Res. Lib. 75 (5), 684—704. Available from: https://doi.org/10.5860/crl.75.5.684.

CHAPTER 10

Space Planning and Off-Site Storage

As ever more information is available electronically, the concept of place-based resources and services is eroded

Hurd (2004)

COST CUTTING

Conserving resources while offering the same services can be considered a new service in which it adds value to the organization. Among the services a library can provide to its parent organization is performing existing operations at a lower cost. Innovative products and services make a splash, but in some cases, research administration would rather see a reduced library budget. If the delivery of reading materials to scientists is the goal, anything to ensure that it can be done at lower cost is worth the science librarian's time, in the opinion of the institutional administration. This has been one of the reasons for the move to demand-driven acquisitions (DDA) in libraries, among other things. Another increasingly appealing option for the library in the opinion of administration is the movement of print collections to off-site storage. The library's central location at many organizations makes it a prime target for relocation so that the space can be used for other things. This is something that many research libraries have faced in the last 20–25 years. Usually viewed as a tragedy by library staff, it can be turned into a positive experience if the effort is well thought through and includes all stakeholders at an early stage.

INEVITABILITY

With reduced visits to central library space, it is only a matter of time before the institutional administration becomes covetous of what appears to them as idle square footage. Science librarians in smaller organizations are familiar with library moves as the need for office, lab, or storage and administrative space regularly trumps the book and journal collection.

Science Libraries in the Self-Service Age
DOI: https://doi.org/10.1016/B978-0-08-102033-3.00010-6

Even when statistics on in-person visits might refute these strategic decisions to move the collection (and library staff), the iconic central library is often shunted off to the side. The recent increase in DDA has meant a slower growth of collections and reduced need for space, yet the trend toward off-site storage facilities is not a fad. Unless digital content proves to be unreliable and there is a large-scale return to print journals by users, the wholesale movement of physical materials to remote buildings will likely continue in favor of alternative uses of the library space.

However, some in the library profession see the value in moving collections to remote storage. The case for freeing up library space is a primary component of David Lewis' strategy for academic libraries in the 21st century. The dean of the Indiana University—Purdue University Library and frequent writer on the future of research libraries says that using prime campus space to house print books and journals which are used less and less is ultimately a losing proposition (Lewis, 2007).

If any research libraries are well positioned to use of remote storage facilities, it is science libraries. The journal-centric nature of collections make for an easy digital-for-print swap and virtually eliminates the common objection to the lack of access to the shelves which is the loss of serendipitous discovery; it may be true that books are discovered accidentally by a user seeking a different title on the shelf, but this is much less likely with journal articles.

PLANNING AND NEGOTIATION

Many who have been through library moves (or drastic reduction in collection and processing space) have faced very short deadlines to vacate their long-held space. And depressing as the prospect is to most library staff, having a plan in place makes the process go more smoothly. It is best for library administration to incorporate this possibility into planning and to get out in front of these moves.

Forward-thinking science librarians might consider negotiating for resources or staff needed to pursue new services in exchange for concessions of real estate (Lewis, 2007). If a chance to participate in the change (even informally) emerges, science librarians should seize the opportunity to present a different scenario to those who ultimately make the decision on space planning. First, a clear message recognizing a reduction in physical visits will acknowledge the inevitable—the library is going to move. But given the opportunity, the librarian should describe the emerging trend of science librarians being inserted into the full research cycle. A description of future support for research data management, institutional publishing efforts, the compliance with funder mandates, and collection of research information reporting and metrics may appeal to administration enough to cultivate dedicated resources for these services in exchange for vacated library space. These new library services can be facilitated by investment in software platforms, training, IT support, and/ or staff development, and all of these can be budgeted as part of the planned facility move. With any collections move, the online catalog will likely need to be updated to reflect new location of materials. Transferring and/or withdrawing materials imply costs of which institutional administration may be wholly unaware, but these should be part of the planning, again with an honest effort by library administration to ameliorate them. Of course, the decision to move the library may be done without library staff input, but where there is room (and enough advanced warning) to influence the planning, librarians may be able to get something in return and should try in any case.

As with many innovations in science libraries, biomedical libraries seem to have led the way in yielding space to the greater organization. This is probably due to the availability of large article repositories such as PubMed Central which make print journals somewhat redundant. Several recent health sciences library moves have been done in cooperation with campus administration which coveted the space for other purposes (Lynn et al., 2011; Tobia and Feldman, 2010; Thibodeau, 2010; Tooey, 2010). If the general experience with science library service innovation is any guide, the health sciences libraries' handling and negotiation of collections space loss will probably be instructive to other science libraries in the future.

TECHNOLOGY AND REMOTE COLLECTIONS

On the surface, cost-savings-as-a-service appears to make most sense in libraries where content is available digitally and since scientific journals online more than most other collection areas, science libraries are prime candidates for being moved. Even where journal back files are not available online, moving older volumes out of the central library and to an off-site storage facility is probably not objectionable since scan-and-send technology is today advanced enough to make it easy to provide access to these resources quickly. And depending on the scientific discipline, journal literature is most valuable when it is current. If the estimated citation half-life of certain journals is low, it may present another justification for moving the run off-site. That's not to say the articles from prior years are no longer useful, only that they are not in high demand relative to other parts of the collection. With digitization tools becoming commonplace, articles can be retrieved in a short time when there is a need.

With much content (especially in the biomedical sciences) delivered in short articles, a digital reproduction of the desired materials is normally good enough for the requesting patron. Certainly, longer works and even whole books can be (and are) scanned and hosted, but the current reluctance to adopt e-readers and the die-hard reliance on PDF as a standard format among scientists means that a method of rapid physical delivery should be planned when considering a collection move off-site. It is possible and even likely that the use of drones for delivery becomes practical, and depending on distance from the off-site storage facility, delivery of materials may be cut down to an hour or so.

Negotiations with the parent organization on possible library enhancements in exchange for space concession might include some investment in an automated storage and retrieval system for the off-site facility. While some existing systems are rather costly, it is likely that innovations in the commercial sector, specifically in retail inventory management and warehouse operations can yield systems with application to library storage facilities. Also, as the use of robots becomes more common, librarians facing collections moves to remote locations might request bids on supplemental systems which could one day assist in the labor-intensive pulling and shelving that off-site storage will inevitably require. Forward-thinking administration may find potential labor cost savings appealing if such a system seems viable.

COOPERATIVE COLLECTION STORAGE

It is often worthwhile to investigate the coordination of collection storage and retention with other research libraries so that costly duplication in handling and space usage can be minimized. With most research libraries facing a space crunch and budget pressures, demonstrating to institutional administration that further cost cutting efforts are being considered by cooperative collection management is a worthwhile endeavor. However, several things must be documented when sharing remote storage space. Libraries considering sharing storage facilities should create and sign agreements or a memorandum of understanding (MOU) on term of service which should specify things such as the division of costs and contingencies for one or the other to exit the facility and the agreement. Sharing off-site storage with another science library may enable further saving where materials are duplicated, and therefore only one copy needs be retained to serve multiple institutions. This is where it gets tricky though since in the event the material is deaccessioned and withdrawn, consortial arrangements should specify which parties are affected and have to formally agree. In any case, the effort at leveraging storage by sharing existing facilities with other libraries is another issue about which institutional administration should be notified as an attempt at cost savings by the library.

COMMUNICATION TO USERS

While many scientists may visit the library less and less frequently with the availability of journals online, it is common to hear objections from them when a transfer of (perhaps little used) print journals is proposed. Nonetheless, it is always best to contact all stakeholders with plans to move collections to off-site storage as early as possible in the process. It is also extremely helpful to have usage statistics for items proposed for relocation. This is often dependent on reshelving counts or for monographs, circulation statistics. But if the impetus to move comes from central administration, librarians can ask for staff or equipment to assist with reshelving counts as a management-information tool. The citation half-life of journals if available is also a measure that is meaningful to scientists—even if only for a group of journals in a broad scientific discipline.

Administration may be pleased with the attempt to save space and money, but scientists may cringe at the idea of withdrawing titles and discarding them. It is best to state the potential scenarios up front and to avoid surprise objections later. It is important to document and communicate these issues, and where possible, any deaccession decisions to institutional stakeholders. Management's desires aside, the creation of prime space in what was once the library for other uses may not be immediately recognized by scientists. However, the emphasis on scan-on-demand and the availability of same-day delivery services can help to reassure scientists who may express resistance to moving collections off the central location.

LIBRARY SPACE

Because of declining visits to the physical library, it is easy to move collections off-site. This gives the institutional administration some options for what is frequently sorely needed space. Many libraries want to retain the space that was once occupied by shelving and use it for other educational purposes such as group study and instructional spaces. The reuse of buildings in this way appears to be a successful model at some institutions. Converting library-shelving areas to study areas, makerspaces, computer labs, and other purposes when cleared of their collections might be most suitable for undergraduate institutions where group study and learning are the norm. But for professional scientists or faculty and their graduate students, these new uses may not be nearly as appealing. It is also increasingly common for university libraries to remove the traditional reference desk in response to declining in-person visits. Librarians in many cases then hold office hours whereby any question is referred to the librarian in his/her office. Other models emphasize embedded librarians where training and other services take place within research teams, labs, or offices of scientists.

SUMMARY

With technology exerting pressure on libraries from all sides, it is understandable that those outside the profession see the relocation of print collections as natural. Indeed, science librarians should become used to the idea, and if they haven't yet been confronted with a proposed move, they should anticipate one. But with a bit of forethought and planning, the disruptive nature of collections moves can be not only alleviated but possibly turned into a positive for emerging science library services. That is, if the value and resource requirements of these new activities can be demonstrated to administration and coupled with the concession of library space.

REFERENCES

Hurd, J., 2004. Scientific communication: new roles and new players. Sci. Technol. Lib. 25 (1/2), 5—22.

Lewis, D.W., 2007. A strategy for academic libraries in the first quarter of the 21st century. Coll. Res. Lib. 68 (5), 418—434.

Lynn, V.A., FitzSimmons, M., Robinson, C.K., 2011. Special report: symposium on transformational change in health sciences libraries: space, collections, and roles. J. Med. Lib. Assoc. 99 (1), 82—87. Available from: http://doi.org/10.3163/1536-5050.99.1.014.

Tobia, R.C., Feldman, J.D., 2010. Making lemonade from lemons: a case study on loss of space at the Dolph Briscoe, Jr. Library, University of Texas Health Science Center at San Antonio. J. Med. Lib. Assoc. Available from: http://doi.org/10.3163/1536-5050.98.1.013.

Thibodeau, P.L., 2010. When the library is located in prime real estate: a case study on the loss of space from the Duke University Medical Center Library and Archives. J. Med. Lib. Assoc. 98 (1), 25–28. Available from: http://doi.org/10.3163/1536-5050.98.1.010.

Tooey, M.J., 2010. Renovated, repurposed, and still "one sweet library": a case study on loss of space from the Health Sciences and Human Services Library, University of Maryland, Baltimore. J. Med. Lib. Assoc. Available from: http://doi.org/10.3163/1536-5050.98.1.014.

CHAPTER 11

Skills and Training

NEED FOR TRAINING

The transition to new services in science libraries does not happen by simply deciding on new forms of user support. Aside from defining, planning, and ensuring the sustainability of these activities, some library staff will need to acquire new knowledge and competencies in order to undertake them adequately (Auckland, 2012). The need for the development of new skills by 21st century research librarians is demonstrated by the creation of the joint Task Force on Librarians' Competencies in Support of E-Research and Scholarly Communication. Formed by the Association of Research Libraries (ARL), the Canadian Association of Research Libraries (CARL), the Association of European Research Libraries (LIBER), and the Confederation of Open Access Repositories (COAR), this task force has worked to identify emerging specialty roles which support new activities in the digital age. The task force is no longer active but published several resources serving as competency profiles for librarians in these new roles.

GENERAL KNOWLEDGE AND SKILLS

Across all new services in science libraries is the need for librarians to have an understanding of the elements of what is commonly called the "research enterprise" and/or the research life cycle. This includes details of what scientists do when not seeking books, articles, or other information from the library. It would be useful for science librarians to know about their users' activities as they happen including hypothesis formation, proposal writing, seeking collaborators and staffing, scheduling laboratory and instrument access, planning necessary travel, collecting and analyzing data, and publishing the results. It is important to remember that for each scientist who visits or otherwise uses the library, s/he is in one or the other of these stages in the research life cycle, and there is an opportunity for the librarian to ask about the process—they are generally glad to share that information. In particular, postdocs or other early-

Science Libraries in the Self-Service Age
DOI: https://doi.org/10.1016/B978-0-08-102033-3.00011-8

career scientists are more likely to interact with the librarian and eager to talk about their work. If science librarians offer an introductory session for new staff, they can inquire about research projects in the pipeline perhaps instead of reviewing services which may have already begun moving in the self-service direction. Familiarity with the research life cycle informs many other services in science libraries today including the ones most discussed in this book.

SPECIFIC COMPETENCIES

All science librarians should know about traditional and open-access publishing models, intellectual property issues, and the economics of scholarly publishing (Schmidt et al., 2016). An interest by librarians in not what the scientists are reading, but what they are writing and where they are publishing often leads to a deeper engagement since this is an important topic to scientists. Science librarians should keep abreast of trends in open access including new entrants into the OA journal space, pricing models, and whether one's scientist-users have published there or are considering it. A knowledge of rights to post reprints as well as the methods and resources to make their works available are critical to science librarians hoping to keep the attention of their user community.

Aside from the publishing activities of scientists, librarians today need to know more about the workings of commonly used discovery service platforms. This goes beyond simply knowing how to perform elaborate searches since increasingly the end user is left to him/herself to use most discovery tools. A knowledge of how metadata is constructed and, most importantly, how it integrates with other systems is critical for librarians to understand and with which to develop some facility. As discovery systems become more modular and metadata content is accepted from a variety of sources, librarians should be prepared to assist in the development of these systems. The use of unique identifiers and their application to research components like publications, datasets, and authors is critical to an understanding and facility with metadata collection and integration.

On the Importance of Identifiers

Among the concepts mentioned throughout this book and that have application to countless new services in science libraries is that of the persistent identifier (PID). These are generally alphanumeric strings that may appear

(Continued)

(Continued)

unintelligible to us but are used extensively to uniquely identify online resources. In some sense, we can consider barcodes to have some of the same characteristics as unique identifiers in which they represent a resource (a book in this case) and its metadata, although not necessarily an online resource. PIDs are emerging in importance throughout the scientific research enterprise as a tool to manage information about research activity and outputs. Knowledge of the many types of PIDs and their application in the research enterprise is therefore highly valuable for science librarians.

A note about taxonomy: in this book, the term, "identifier" is used to refer to globally unique identifiers, persistent identifiers, unique identifiers, digital object identifiers and any unique string that is actionable as a hyperlink and resolves to a web page describing a research outputs, scholars or resources.

What Is a Persistent Identifier (PID)? The management of online metadata is made much more easy when the resource described by the metadata is unambiguously identified. PIDs are cryptic representations of these resources, and they allow the easy transfer of metadata between and among systems which collect and store information about them. PIDs today are created to represent not only online publications but scholar/authors, funding agencies, research awards, and, more recently, facilities and laboratories with which scientists perform their work. To science librarians, the most familiar PID today is the DOI associated with an article.

PIDs are globally unique in that they are not duplicated or reused. This allows them to be used in database management since matching on an item's identifier (rather than author names and titles which can vary) ensures that duplicates are not added or are identified and removed. PIDs are unique in part because they are associated with a web domain and normally presented as a hyperlink. This in turn makes PIDs actionable in that they bring a user to a web resource/page representing the resource. The article DOI is familiar to science librarians in this form: https://doi.org/10.1126/science.1194442.

The creation of links using PIDs is important not only to present a description or view of the metadata and its resource, but it is also used to make the hyperlink permanent. The persistence of PIDs is important since web pages sometimes move or have their URL changed, but the management of PIDs means that the identifier will remain constant and the URL to which it points can be updated when/if the resource URL changes. Several studies have shown "link rot" among online scientific web pages, but the PID is designed to reduce or eliminate this—provided they are maintained.

(Continued)

(Continued)
Who Uses PIDs?

PIDs are used by publishers and research organizations to easily refer to an object that might otherwise take a good deal of text to describe. An example would be a publication: a human-readable description would include coauthors, title, date of publication, pagination, and several other elements. But a PID represents the publication by using a single string of letters and/or numbers. Increasingly, funding agencies, journal publishers, and others with an interest in collecting data about research activity are incorporating PIDs into their online systems since they are universally recognized and ensure that data is interoperable with other elements of the scientific research community.

Where Are PIDs Used?

PIDs are found throughout the research enterprise. They are used to uniquely identify publications, datasets, individual scholars, funding agencies, and, perhaps soon, a host of other scholarly entities including labs, instruments, and specimens. One can see them on reference lists as DOIs accompanying citations or as ORCIDs appearing on a scientist's web page and/or the landing page of an article in an electronic journal. More importantly for the automation and integration of research information, PIDs are used behind the scenes, for example, on the CrossRef or ORCID web platforms where they are exposed for machine-to-machine communication, linking people, publications, grants, funding, and other elements of the research cycle. The creation of open application programming interface (APIs) which incorporate identifiers offers tremendous opportunities to leverage this data

What Are PIDs Used For?

Publishers have recognized the value of identifiers in managing their content, and librarians have adopted them in their work. Identifiers not only provide a stable link to an online resource (thereby circumventing link rot) but very often are created as a representation of a rich source of metadata that describes the resource and that can be integrated into other online systems. PIDs are helpful not only in enabling machine-to-machine communication but in disambiguating resources that might otherwise be confused. An example might be versions of a research dataset both of which have the same title, creator, file formats, etc. and are indistinguishable except for a version number. Similarly, researchers who share the same first and last name might only be differentiated by their ORCID.

These strings of characters are mostly unintelligible to anyone who comes across them in print, but they are very powerful when used in machine-to-machine communication. In addition, many identifier issuing bodies have set

(*Continued*)

(Continued)

up rather robust APIs to allow users to retrieve and reuse information about the resource being identified (bibliographic data about an article, in the case of CrossRef DOIs).

One advantage of identifiers is in not only uniquely identifying resources with similar names (as with ORCIDs to disambiguate authors) but also they can help in measuring impact in that clicks on an actionable identifier in order to view the online resource can be counted and quantified either over time or in comparison with other resources using PIDs.

Persistent, unique identifiers are also crucial to participate in what many are seeing as the next great thing in information science—linked data. This is a way of constructing metadata that makes it both machine and human readable, and allowing easy integration into other systems that use linked data. A common example of linked data is DBpedia, a representation of Wikipedia as linked data.

Use of PIDs in Libraries

Science librarians who develop or assist with the creation of local databases documenting research activity (including institutional repositories) should look for the use of PIDs by other systems and incorporate them into their local database where possible. This ensures that the data can be integrated with other services. This would also apply to maintaining information about authors by incorporating the ORCID identifier. Certainly, any effort to implement institutional license to metrics tools such as Altmetric or PlumX would be made much easier with the use of identifiers for publications, scholars, and perhaps institutions/departments.

ORCID, OCLC, NISO, and other organizations regularly offer webinars on the topics related to the use of PIDs.

Many librarians recognize the broader issues around the need to share research data to leverage today's scientific research in support of future inquiry. However, there may be a common reluctance to delve too deeply into learning more or acquiring skills in this area due to unfamiliarity with or misunderstanding of the mechanics of data management (Bresnahan and Johnson, 2013). There might also be a misconception that providing data-management services requires some intermediate (or advanced) IT or technical skills. While technical or subject knowledge is helpful, most librarians who explore research data-management services will see that the terms and concepts are analogous to those they may have learned in standard cataloging and classification courses.

Research data aside, science librarians who begin to offer services in research information management—including the collection and sharing of bibliographic data outside the traditional library catalog—should familiarize themselves with established formats and procedures. An understanding of relational databases, queries, and markup languages can go a long way in explaining how the collection of institutionally created research outputs can go more smoothly. It is helpful to be able to read HTML and perhaps CSS or inline style markup. For example, when viewing the source data for a web page and/or displayed search results, it is easier to find and understand how the data is structured and shown to the end user. Copying the URL which appears when a search is done and experimenting with changing the variables to create a new search is an example of something that can be easily learned and a handy skill to have. With some exploration of URL syntax, predetermined searches can be executed with a hyperlink in and embedded on web pages to get a user right to the information s/he needs.

While not essential for science librarians to master, file formats such as comma or tab delimited, XML and JSON are illustrative of how descriptive and administrative metadata is created and integrated with other systems. Along with these formats is an understanding that computers and servers routinely share information without human intervention. Commonly referred to as APIs, the automated exchange of bibliographic data or other research information (e.g., through the exposure of a repository's data via OAI-PMH) is something that science librarians should be aware of—but not necessarily experts in. Simply being aware that conversion of metadata to XML or JSON is enough to ensure that it is continually synchronized with other systems, websites and services without the need to manually copy and move data is sufficient. Reformatting data in this way makes it possible for librarians to partner with other units and effectively participate in organization-wide research information collection and sharing.

The familiar use of an ASCII text editor (not a word processor) to manipulate URLs and/or view files is also useful in developing these capacities. There are several low cost or freely available text editors which display content as color coded or indented for ease of reading depending on the file format and extension. Similarly, plugins are available for some browsers that will open files of these and other formats for ease of viewing. While these formats are primarily created with the intention of machine-to-machine communication, tools that make them easily viewable make the job of understanding this part of the research infra-structure a bit easier.

PROJECT MANAGEMENT

A critical need for science librarians today is not so much a specific skill as a service orientation. The acquisition of research materials from outside the organization and the development of a comprehensive subject collection meet a user need that is in decline. These books and journals formally produced and distributed by commercial and other professional publishers are becoming available directly to the reader, bypassing the library-as-gatekeeper. What is emerging is the reverse: the collection of research materials produced *within* the research organization for dissemination to outside users. This is what OCLC's Lorcan Dempsey calls "inside-out" libraries.

Librarians who engage in the inside-out library will soon find themselves involved in projects with multiple players, some outside of the library. Conversion of text to digital, metadata markup, management of open-source platforms on space provided by the organization's IT office all require the coordination of activity among library staff as well as contractors, webmasters, and creators of the content. Librarians should have some grasp of project-management principles. And while they need not be certified as such, the more knowledge gained in the basic steps and procedures of project management, the more likely the science librarian is to have success in the endeavor.

LEARNING METHODS

Unfortunately, there does not seem to be a great deal of emphasis on scholarly communications in today's library and information science (LIS) programs (Bonn, 2014). The same may be true for teaching more specific skills such as repository management, copyright advisory, and open-access issues although the discrepancy is understandable given the relatively recent emergence of these programs (Simons and Richardson, 2012; Finlay et al., 2015). Because of a general lack of formal training opportunities in many of these areas, it is likely that science librarians who acquire the skills and knowledge required to provide expanded researcher support services will either be self-taught or learn via informal and internal opportunities. Just as many people use Google to answer questions once directed to the library reference desk, librarians can likewise help themselves to training opportunities freely available online.

Individuals and communities with expertise in those new service categories use Listservs and social media channels to disseminate relevant knowledge, and their presence has grown in recent years. In addition, many organizations with an interest in expanded library support for the research enterprise have posted guides, curricula, and other resources online. A list of online resources which may be of interest is appended to this chapter.

EXISTING COMPETENCIES

Finally, librarians already possess one of the most valuable skills required in the development of new service categories: the ability to learn independently. Librarians are familiar with a wide range of search tools and resources to easily identify material on a certain topic and to sift through to find the most relevant, concise, and accessible for learning purposes. The compilation of instructional materials on science libraries in the digital era is a trivial task for librarians and makes the acquisition of knowledge and competencies much easier.

Development of competence and skills in a particular area is often much more effective when the learner has practical exercises to which they can apply the newly acquired knowledge. For that reason, it is not unusual for new services to launch with support by library staff who are as yet novices in the area but for whom the day-to-day operations make more sense as time goes on. The old saying admonishes us not to "get it right" but simply to "get it going" and expect improvement to come with experience.

RESOURCES

Curriculum

UNESCO Open Access Curriculum for Researchers and Library Schools.http://www.unesco.org/new/en/communication-and-information/resources/publications-and-communication-materials/publications/publications-by-series/oa-curricula-for-researchers-and-library-schools/

Organizations Offering Training Material, Webinars, and Videos

Coalition for Networked Information (CNI)

Data Curation Center (DCC)

Library Juice Academy

Scholarly Publishing and Academic Resources Coalition (SPARC)

National Information Standards Organization (NISO)

Listservs and Other Online Communities

Scholcomm (Association of College and Research Libraries) Listserv

Liblicense (Center for Research Libraries) Listserv

RDAP (Research Data Access and Preservation) Listserv

JISC-Repositories Listserv

IR Managers Forum (See: https://groups.google.com/forum/#! forum/irmanagers)

KnowledgeSpeak Newsletter

LIS-E-Resources Listserv

ASIS&T Listserv

Digital Science (Blog and Twitter Feed)

REFERENCES

Auckland, M., 2012. Re-skilling for skilling for research: an investigation into the role and skills of subject and liaison librarians required to effectively support the evolving information needs of researchers. RLUK. Retrieved from <http://www.rluk.ac.uk/content/re-skilling-research>.

Bonn, M., 2014. Tooling up: scholarly communication education and training. Coll. Res. Libr. News 75 (3), 132–135.

Bresnahan, M.M., Johnson, A.M., 2013. Assessing scholarly communication and research data training needs. Ref. Serv. Rev. Available from: http://doi.org/10.1108/RSR-01-2013-0003.

Finlay, C., Tsou, A., Sugimoto, C., 2015. Scholarly communication as a core competency: prevalence, activities, and concepts of scholarly communication librarianship as shown through job advertisements. J. Librarianship Scholar. Commun. 3 (1), eP1236. Available from: http://doi.org/10.7710/2162-3309.1236.

Schmidt, B., Calarco, P., Kuchma, I., Shearer, K., 2016. Time to adopt: librarians' new skills and competency profiles. In: Loizides, F., Schmidt, B. (Eds.), Positioning and Power in Academic Publishing: Players, Agents and Agendas. IOS Press, Amsterdam, pp. 1–8.

Simons, N., Richardson, J., 2012. New roles, new responsibilities: examining training needs of repository staff. J. Librarianship Scholarly Commun. 1 (2), eP1051. Available from: http://doi.org/10.7710/2162-3309.1051.

CHAPTER 12

Summary: The Inevitability of the Self-Service Model

Someday those of us born before 1985 or so may tell our children and grandchildren about the way we used to watch movies in the late 20th century. We might tell them, "At one time, when you wanted to watch a movie, you had to get in the car and drive to a store and get a DVD or video tape and pay a rental fee for it." If we don't get sidetracked by a discussion of what DVD and VHS are, we might continue, "you had to return it in 7 days and if it was a tape, you had to rewind it or face an additional fee." And further, "If the movie you wanted was already rented to someone else, you had to come back later and hope it was there. Occasionally you found a movie that you hadn't heard of before and you ended up liking it. Kind of like finding a book in a library that you didn't know about until you were looking for something else."

And these 21st-century children may look at us like we're from another planet.

They may ask what happened to all that and we will go on to explain that these "video stores," as they were known eventually, went away when it became cheap and easy enough to send movies over the Internet and to collect payment from viewers.

The movie, television, newspaper, and music industries were blindsided by digital distribution, and they will never be the same. It is important to note in this story that a number of employees in the media industry lost their jobs during this transition. A lot of who were probably decent people worked in video stores; they were often helpful and knew a lot of movies that they sometimes recommended to us. But it wasn't just the video store clerks who had to find something else to do. Anyone involved in the distribution, warehousing, ordering, billing, promotion, property management, and other functions related to running a video-rental enterprise found themselves out of work overnight when movies were delivered directly to users.

It might be that the last area of media to be affected by digital delivery is scholarly publishing. Perhaps due to its reverence for the established,

Science Libraries in the Self-Service Age
DOI: https://doi.org/10.1016/B978-0-08-102033-3.00012-X

traditional publication system and hide-bound practices, the business model of scholarly publishing has only faced disruptive change after the inefficiencies of most other media businesses have been wrung out. Some say it is ironic that the Internet was developed by and for scientists but they are the last to exploit its full potential in scientific communication. But in any case, because scholarly publishing is a laggard among other media, science librarians might have a chance to get out in front of the changes and at least take some control over what might happen.

Librarians may be better positioned to adapt to new distribution models of research publications than video stores and other commercial enterprises. A long-term relationship with their users and their parent organization as well as the relatively slow change and adherence to tradition in scholarly publishing may turn out to be a factor in saving libraries and librarians—provided they can react quickly enough. However, science librarians have to accept that scientists can and do retrieve a large body of articles themselves, without the need to visit the library. This understanding should give the science librarian enough lead time to develop nontraditional services and remain relevant to the research enterprise and perhaps avoid the fate of those who worked in other media-based businesses.

Institutional repositories, metrics services, and library-publishing initiatives are some of the early efforts to anticipate these changes and adapt quickly enough to provide value to the organization before any hasty decision to eliminate the library can be brought by budget pressures.

It is not inevitable that science libraries go the way of the video store. After all, one is a nonprofit and mostly owned and operated by a larger entity, whereas the other is for profit and had to stand on its own financial support. But what is inevitable is the movement of mediated services to self-service in nearly all enterprises: commercial, nonprofit, educational, or entertainment.

INDEX

Printed and bound by CPI Group (UK) Ltd, Croydon, CR0 4YY

08/06/2025

01896869-0008